T0357340

Praise for *What Must Be Carried*

"Whitney gives an honest reflection on grief that empowers readers to move forward, discovering that even in the darkest moments, joy and authenticity are within reach."

—David Ferrugio
creator of DEAD Talks Podcast

"Whitney's *What Must Be Carried* offers a powerful reminder that healing isn't about returning to what once was, but rather creating space in our hearts for what is. Her writing beautifully encourages us to unapologetically embrace every emotion, allowing us to honor our grief while simultaneously seeking peace and joy. As a fellow young widow, I feel truly blessed by her wisdom in this guide. Whitney instills hope, reminding us that the power to heal lies within, and that What Must Be Carried won't always feel this heavy. She is a true gift to anyone walking the path of profound loss."

—Krystina Dinardo
widow, mother of three, and digital content creator

"Despite being written while in hell, Whitney's words offer a soft balm for all human hearts. She paints a realistic portrait of loss and grief—one of despair but also hope."

—Stacey Heale
author of Now Is Not the Time for Flowers

"As a fellow young widow, Whitney truly does an amazing job articulating what life after loss looks like. Her ability to tackle the raw and messy parts of grief without sugar-coating it is undoubtedly valuable. By offering practical and tangible ways to navigate through dark times, she provides a sense of hope and empowerment, allowing the reader to find their own path to healing. In this book, Whitney's passion for helping others is palpable, while offering gentle guidance that supports you on your own journey."

—Kellie Bullard-Kelley
author of Behind My Smile

What Must Be Carried

What Must Be Carried

Living a Beautiful Life Beyond Loss

Whitney Lyn Allen Gadecki

JB JOSSEY-BASS™
A Wiley Brand

Published by John Wiley & Sons, Inc., Hoboken, New Jersey.
Published simultaneously in Canada.

For general information on our other products and services or for technical support, please contact our Customer Care Department within the United States at (800) 762-2974, outside the United States at (317) 572-3993 or fax (317) 572-4002.

Wiley also publishes its books in a variety of electronic formats. Some content that appears in print may not be available in electronic formats. For more information about Wiley products, visit our web site at www.wiley.com.

Library of Congress Cataloging-in-Publication Data

Names: Gadecki, Whitney Lyn Allen, author.
Title: What must be carried : living a beautiful life beyond loss / Whitney Lyn Allen Gadecki.
Description: [San Francisco, California]: Jossey-Bass, [2025]
Identifiers: LCCN 2024042400 (print) | LCCN 2024042401 (ebook) | ISBN 9781394311996 (hardback) | ISBN 9781394312016 (adobe pdf) | ISBN 9781394312009 (epub)
Subjects: LCSH: Grief. | Death—Psychological aspects.
Classification: LCC BF575.G7 G355 2025 (print) | LCC BF575.G7 (ebook) | DDC 155.9/37—dc23/eng/20241125
LC record available at https://lccn.loc.gov/2024042400
LC ebook record available at https://lccn.loc.gov/2024042401

Cover Design: Paul McCarthy
Cover Art: © Getty Images | Kampee Patisena   SKY10096039_011025

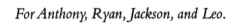

For Anthony, Ryan, Jackson, and Leo.

Contents

Letter to the Reader

While I was waiting at a local coffee shop for the funeral director down the street to text me to pick up my handsome husband's ashes and the documents solidifying his death to the world, I sat and drank my iced Americano and stared blankly at the people passing. Many were smiling and laughing. Some were sitting at nearby tables with their headphones on, intently gazing at their computer screens. Life was happening all around me and I wanted to scream, *"Don't you fucking see me?! My husband is dead! Look at me damn it!"* There were people that locked eyes with me for a brief moment and smiled but they didn't **really** see me. I felt like I was alone in a world where no one could understand what it felt like to have the person that you planned forever with be ripped away. I felt like a stranger in my own body, feeling emotions I didn't even know I had the capacity to feel, in a world that no longer made sense to me. The pain and the trauma

I endured felt invisible. I was a living ghost. And without possessing the knowledge and tools yet of how to manage the weight of my loss, I felt like I was suffocating and crumbling underneath of it all. I felt like I had reached rock bottom, but this is where starting over after Ryan's death really began for me. It is where my processing, self-evaluation, and healing began. It is literally where I started to write my first book, *Running in Trauma Stilettos*, but also where I was symbolically starting to write the next chapter of my life without my husband and father of our two children, Jackson and Leo. I knew sitting in that coffee shop while I waited for the funeral director to text me, that resenting the happy and carefree people around me was not the answer, although at the time, those emotions wrapped themselves around me like a warm, soft blanket, comforting and soothing me. But this didn't feel like living at all. It felt like suffering.

★★★

I was in a dark place then, so dark in fact that my body and mind were numb to the pain the majority of the time. If our bodies and minds allowed us to feel the enormity of the pain that crashes into us when we endure such loss all at once, it would certainly wreak such havoc on our systems that we could die of a broken heart. I was grateful for the numbness. When my mind and body did allow me to feel anything, my "go-to" emotion was rage, which hid the intensity of the agony underneath. I had to release the anger and guilt I was holding, at myself, at the world, at Ryan for dying and leaving me a young widow with two young children. I had to learn to carry my loss, my pain, and my grief so it didn't feel like it was all-consuming. I had to learn to integrate Ryan's absence from my life and my future and still find joy, beauty, and purpose in the world. Somehow feeling at rock bottom was the catalyst for beginning to rebuild my life from the ashes. This meant figuring out how to adapt, grow, and evolve in my own grief to transform and tame the darkness that was crushing me so I could feel like I was still living life with it. It meant discovering what life looked like for me now in a world where my husband was dead.

Perhaps you were drawn to this book because you find yourself in a dark place similar to how I just described it. A hole that feels so dark, dreary, and monumental that you can't even fathom your first step toward the light. I have since learned that finding yourself in this exquisitely painful purgatory between your old life and the life that you could live is part of surviving a life-altering loss.

Whereas my first book, *Running in Trauma Stilettos*, is a retelling of the trials and tribulations I had to endure between the time of Ryan suffering an anoxic brain injury from a freak severe allergic reaction to a bee sting, to the time of his death, this book is different. My first book was a way for others going through the worst days of their lives to feel seen and witnessed in what they are experiencing or had experienced in a real and raw way. This book is a compilation of the experiences I have been through after Ryan's death in order to show you how to build something beautiful out of something traumatic and messy. It is a collection of lessons I have learned throughout my time as a widow that have allowed me to hold my grief as I go through life and write this new chapter without the person that I was supposed to be with until the end of my story. This book is my way of showing you that there is life worth living on the other side of loss.

***

When Ryan was on hospice before his death on April 7, 2022, my time away from "death watch," as I called it, was my weekly therapy sessions with a grief counselor. During one of our sessions, I asked my therapist a simple question as I stared out the window feeling exhaustion to my bones, "Will I ever feel content again?" It sounded like a simple enough question, but it was complicated. It was so many questions wrapped into one. I was asking if I would ever feel joy, security, and safety again. I was asking: "Can I not only survive this, but can I heal enough to find peace again? Will I feel normal again? Can I love my life again? Can I find beauty in this life when I hold all this ugliness now? At thirty-five years old is my life just downhill from here? Will it always feel this damn heavy?" I don't remember how she answered my question and it wouldn't have mattered. Even if she had said the most insightful thing on Earth, I wouldn't have believed her. I was completely enveloped by darkness and death, literally watching my beautiful husband wither away and die before my very eyes a short ten-minute drive from where I sat that day. My "break" was talking about how fucked up it all was. Any potential future life for me that was close to something that looked like contentment didn't seem possible. I wish that I could have known what I know now, that the gravity of the grief that I held then will feel differently as time passes and I create a new reality and version of myself and life. That the sheer force of it all isn't as insurmountable as I once honestly believed. There is contentment to be found when you come to peace with the fact that life now demands holding so much all at once: the pain of your loss, the love for your person that is no longer here, and the joy and purpose that you are able to find in the aftermath. I know it may seem like any semblance of happiness and meaning is an impossibility at the moment. The truth is, there will never be life without grief now, but that can be seen as both a burden and a privilege if you allow it to. You see, I have discovered that I will always carry the pain of losing my husband, Ryan, but grief has also allowed me to live more authentically. Grief has given me the courage to live more urgently and go after my new ambitions and purpose in a fearless way, including leaving my ten-year career as an attorney to pursue helping others in grief through writing about loss and also by becoming a certified grief educator. Ryan's death was a slap in the face and a harsh reminder that life is painfully short and I refused to continue any career that didn't make me feel fulfilled. Helping others navigate their own grief and showing how they can take back their power that death steals from them, feels authentic to the transformed person I have become as a result of Ryan's death. Grief has allowed me to cherish every beautiful moment and everyone in my life more fully. I want to remind you that losing your person is unfair. Having to endure trauma and heartache like you've endured is unfair. But the lessons that can flow as a consequence of living through the darkness of grief and death and the meaning it can bring to your life in the aftermath can be a gift if you allow yourself to truly see and feel it. It isn't all bad. Life is never all bad. There is beauty to be found among the wreckage of a broken life and heart, but you have to first believe you deserve to find the light again. I know what is possible for you because I have found contentment and solace in my life after loss and this book is a guide on how you can balance holding all of these emotions and experiences with more ease and grace so you can start living again.

A New Chapter

It is just past 5:30 a.m. in the morning and the light is beginning to peak in through the floor-to-ceiling windows in the living room. I am sitting in a large, plush, cream-colored chaise sipping on freshly brewed Nespresso trying to drink away my early morning grogginess. I am not living in the home that my husband and I shared and had planned to raise our family in when he was alive. I am living in a new home with my two sweet boys and a man that I fell in love with shortly and unexpectedly after my husband's death. His name is Anthony. Anthony is peaceful, patient, kind, understanding, and thoughtful. We have committed to building a life together, which includes an engagement, marriage, and hopefully growing our family in the future. He is the first person who really saw me for me after becoming a widow, and he has been my grounding force since we met in June 2022. We are building a life together in all its beauty and messiness. I am not numb, angry, resentful, or full of despair like I was more than a year ago. I am not in a dark place like I once was in the immediate aftermath of Ryan's death. Ryan is still gone and I miss him terribly. The mere passage of time is painful because I am getting farther away from when I last heard his voice or laugh, or I felt his hug or kiss.

My children are growing and becoming little people with big personalities and I wish he could be part of it. My heart will always ache that he isn't here to experience life with us. These things will always bear weight on my soul and none of it can be changed. And I've found contentment and solace. I've come to peace and acceptance that there are irreconcilable things in life that can never be made better or fixed and I have learned to live with these harsh and painful realities and find the beauty in life. All of these things are true at once. By living with grief after a life-altering loss, we discover that so many truths and emotions can be true at once. And we carry them all.

You may be reading this right now and are holding the belief that joy, contentment, purpose, and seeing the beauty and magic in life is beyond your grasp after the death of your person. Your chest feels tight and like at any moment your heart could just burst into a million pieces. As you walk it feels like there is cement in your shoes and every time you open your mouth to speak, a lump in your throat forms that impedes you from speaking without your voice cracking and tears streaming down your face. Grief makes us feel out of control and powerless. It takes away every ounce of the magic that we once possessed in our everyday lives. And the most fucked up thing about it all is that we didn't ask for this. We didn't choose to carry this darkness with us, the darkness chose us because life is random, unjust, and unfair at times. But I know if you're reading these words right now that you lived a beautiful life in the "before," in the world before your loss. You know what that can feel like and you deserve to discover what a beautiful life looks like for you now as a person who has suffered a great tragedy. Your new life will look different and even feel differently than it once did, but it can still light your heart on fire. I understand you can't imagine this right now, because I didn't think that I could create anything that resembled anything close to beautiful after Ryan's death because he was so much of what made my life simply enchanting. But I promise it is possible because I've created a new life from the ashes of my pain and deepest heartbreak. The magnitude of the darkness that burdens you now can become lighter. I've learned a lot since my husband's accident. I've learned the ugliness and hopelessness that I can possess. But most profoundly, I've discovered that making life beautiful again by learning to hold and honor my deep loss while still living life to my fullest capacity is a battle worth fighting for. Your battle begins right now. Let's begin discovering what you need to learn to create a beautiful life after a life-altering loss.

Introduction

There is life before your person dies and there is life after. This abrupt shift feels like falling head-first into a deep, dark hole with no bottom. I'm here because I've lost someone precious to me, my husband of eight years, Ryan. I carry a lot with me each day; the weight of Ryan's death is palpable. Ryan was my best friend, the father of my two children, my protector, my sounding board, my entertainment, and my comedian. His soul was larger than life. He was so much of what made my life beautiful and worth living in my "before," and now he is dead. If you're reading this, you've probably lost someone very precious to you too. You may be feeling like you're aimlessly going through the motions of life because the death of your person weighs so heavily that it is all you can feel and think about. You're likely devastated, overwhelmed, and anxious about moving forward in life without the person you love. You may be feeling guilty and confused about how advancing in life is even possible because it feels like grief has put up a huge wall in front of you that you can't tear down. Building a new life around your grief may even be inconceivable for you at the moment. Maybe you've lost hope that happiness and peace are even something you can possess after you've been through the gauntlet of tragedy and trauma. You are apathetic that there is life happening around you because the person you love isn't here to share it with you. This is what a life-altering loss feels like. It is all-consuming and it is the type of loss that has no finality or fixing. Your person is dead and there is no mending that harsh reality. There is no putting a pretty bow around the traumas that are associated with that loss. If you're like me, you've likely seen and experienced things that have brought you to your knees and will forever haunt your soul. There is no silver lining for the fallout that occurs when someone dies and you have to figure out how to pick up the pieces and somehow make pieces of your old life make sense in an entirely different one.

There are things in life (thankfully very few) that cannot be made whole by money, time, platitudes, therapy, flowers, self-care, or sympathy cards. The death of the person you built a life with and wanted to grow old with, or another beloved person in your life, cannot be made whole because there is no suitable substitute or remedy for this. This is a truth that we are tasked to live with and an actuality that will not be OK forever. **And it is OK that this terrible reality will never be OK, because it shouldn't be.** You may be thinking at this point that this is some depressing and dark shit this girl is talking about and *"Great, I am reading this book to feel better and it just sounds like I am screwed here."* And yes, this is some really sad shit I am talking about, but you are not doomed. You may have experienced the most devastating loss, but you are not doomed to live out the rest of your days in misery. The best days of your life are not over if you don't want them to be. In fact, more "best" days are within your reach and possible for you.

The trauma from the experiences I have lived since my husband's accident in October 2021 cannot be disposed of or eliminated. It is part of what has molded me into the woman I am today. It is part of every cell of my being. The memories of these experiences cannot be taken up by anyone else but me; they are mine to hold and bear. They must be carried. My grief used to feel like I was carrying a boulder with me everywhere I went. Ryan's absence from this world was my singular focus because the weight was so great, the crushing nature of it all was so palpable. It was debilitating and destabilizing. But I've learned to hold my grief as I go through life and have discovered how to survive this inconceivable loss. Since Ryan's death, I have experienced new things, created new memories, found new purpose and meaning from my loss, formed new relationships and ended others that didn't serve me, set boundaries, and formed a new identity as someone who is now living as a person who has suffered a life-altering loss. After Ryan's death, I felt a calling to help guide and navigate others who have suffered a life-altering loss. I became a certified grief educator, and now I work one-on-one with other widows and grievers and help them discover how to hold their pain in a way that feels manageable so they can start living a life they love while tending to their grief authentically, given their unique experience. I have traveled, I launched my first book, I have celebrated holidays with Anthony's family, who now feel like family to me and my sons, I have started new traditions, I have weathered several intense waves of grief, I have mothered by myself and have learned to co-parent with Anthony. I have made mistakes and I have triumphed. I have fallen and have picked myself up countless times. I have coped in healthy and unhealthy ways. I have cried, screamed, cursed, laughed, and loved. It has felt like I have lived a hundred years in just over two. That's the thing about living through grief and trauma. Grief, trauma, and death change you indelibly and profoundly. They age your soul and your spirit. They force you to learn lessons and be transformed in a manner that does not equate to the amount of time in days, hours, or minutes that have gone by. You cannot count your worst days on a calendar or clock. I am a different Whitney than the one that was married to Ryan. I have been changed in both beautiful and ugly ways, in ways that only can occur when you completely break, unravel, and build anew from the ashes of a life that no longer exists.

And because of all of this, the weight of my loss has lessened, softened, and quieted. Now my grief feels like I'm carrying around small pebbles in my pocket instead of a boulder. I can feel them jiggle as I go throughout life and sometimes I take them out to hold, but I am truly able to live again. That doesn't mean I don't miss or long for Ryan. It doesn't mean that I don't get filled with rage at how unfair Ryan's accident and death is. At times I still feel deep longing, pain, anger, frustration, and a multitude of other emotions because grief is forever evolving and changing. Grief ebbs and flows with the seasons and with dates that hold significance to your specific loss. For me that is Ryan's and my wedding anniversary (October 12), the day of Ryan's accident (October 14), the day he went home on hospice, and also our anniversary of meeting

(St. Patrick's Day, March 17), the day he died (April 7), his birthday (May 21), and many other milestones throughout the year that are a reminder of his absence.

But my grief no longer controls my world. And if you're reading this, I want that for you too. I want you to be able to honor your loss and be able to lean into the pain when you need to feel it, but I also want you to take intentional steps forward to build a beautiful life. I want the weight that you're feeling on your chest to lift. I want the lump in your throat to dissipate and a calmness, contentment, and feeling of safety to return to your world. And it is possible. More importantly, you deserve to live a meaningful life filled with joy after all the suffering you've endured, although you may feel completely undeserving of these things at the moment.

I want to solidify that if you're reading this that you're in the right place. You're reading these words at the exact moment in time that you need to. This I am certain of. This book is for those individuals living and breathing a reality that they didn't ask for, where their beloved was ripped away from them. This book is for those that live within the confines of a world, after having suffered a life-altering loss that is irreconcilable, but still want to find a way to move forward with this truth and build a beautiful life. It is for those who want to learn to carry a weight that can never be thrown away, but can be carried with more ease as your world becomes less consumed by grief.

This book is not a "how-to," but it will take you through a journey of many experiences, emotions, challenges, and triumphs I went through after my husband's death that I have found are common among other widows and those who have lost someone precious to them. I will add insight and include tools and strategies that I have used myself in my own lived experience as well as learned through becoming a certified grief educator, to build a life around my grief. It will give you permission to feel whatever you are feeling and encourage and empower you to take steps forward even if you're afraid. It will perhaps make you feel better about doing things that you want to do but are hesitant to do because you're nervous that people will judge you. It will allow you to see that starting over isn't about getting it all right or always doing the "healthy" thing, but rather that the process of healing is really messy, imperfect, and comes with a lot of pain. I promise to be real and transparent about what this experience has been like. I certainly don't have all the answers, but if this book can make you feel less alone or you can take some lessons I have learned along the way and implement them into your own life in your own grief journey to help you move forward, then this book is doing exactly what it is intended to do. It is a privilege to be part of this journey with you and my promise to you is that if you take the advice in this book seriously and put it into action in your own life even when it is painful and hard, then the weight you are feeling at this moment won't always feel so heavy.

Grief Is "My Thing" Now

Before Ryan's accident in October 2021, in my life before loss and obviously before the thought of becoming a grief coach was even thought of, I was a lawyer. Specifically, I was a medical malpractice defense attorney. I spent my days answering pleadings, writing briefs, and memoranda, and reading and summarizing thousands upon thousands of pages of medical records. I had been doing this work for almost a decade and although I wouldn't have called it my "life's work," I was good at it and for the most part, I enjoyed it. It was stable and predictable, although also stressful. I was perfectly content working a 9–5 job; supporting Ryan, who was excelling in his dream job as a K9 officer at his police department at the time of his accident; and being a mom to our son, Jackson, and soon our baby, Leo. We had a normal, beautiful, boring life, and I was filled with gratitude for the life Ryan and I had built together. And then it all fell apart on October 14, 2021. Ryan's brain injury caused me to lose the man I loved and to lose so many pieces of myself. After Ryan died, going back to work as an attorney didn't make sense to me anymore. Grief and trauma had completely diminished my capacity for life and simple daily tasks, and therefore returning to a fast-paced and stressful work environment where my grief could not be held and honored because there would be deadlines to meet and clients to keep happy felt overwhelming, if not impossible. Returning to work I had done when Ryan was alive and well, in a world where our family and future were still intact, felt completely inauthentic and incongruous with my new reality. So like the new diamond necklace I purchased as a "my husband is dead" gift to myself and as a symbol of entering a new chapter in my life, I ventured out to discover what felt right and good for me as the new person that had been born from the ashes of grief.

It felt like my calling after Ryan's death was to begin educating the world about what grief, trauma, and starting over after loss really looks like. I wanted to open up a

dialog about young widowhood and the array of emotions
that come with the grief experience but are rarely talked
about in our mainstream culture because they are uncomfortable, painful, and messy. There are so many aspects of
grief that are misunderstood. There is so much ignorance
and fear around the experience that I felt called to expose
the world to it. I gave up practicing law to pursue work as
a certified grief educator because it felt aligned with my
new identity as a person who had gone through a life-
altering lossI wanted to help others through the worst days
of their lives and become the person and resource I needed
when my own grief felt suffocating. After Ryan died, I
desperately looked for books, podcasts, and other resources
that captured the intensity of the experience I was walking
through. It seemed like all the books and resources on
grief that I found missed the mark on exposing the raw-
ness and ugliness of it all. The resources I found didn't talk
about the realities of seeing someone die or being left a
young widow and all the secondary losses and fallout that
come with the death of a spouse. Everything I found simply scratched the surface, which left me feeling alone, iso-
lated, and completely unwitnessed in my grief. I came to
the conclusion that there just aren't enough tangible
resources available that capture the sometimes hard and
provocative truths about living with grief. This book is my
way of sharing what it is truly like to walk through hell
and take back your power in a situation that can leave you
feeling powerless, so no one ever has to feel alone and
hopeless like I once did.

I also began sharing the realities of living with grief on
social media so others going through the same pain wouldn't

have to feel alone. What first began as sharing Ryan's health updates on Facebook to close family, friends, and colleagues became sharing truths about grief and trauma to a community of thousands across multiple social media platforms. I hate that grief is "my thing" now because it is only my thing because my husband is dead. But this is also my life and it feels like a sacred privilege for people to come to me in the depths of their despair and at their most vulnerable. I became the person to sit in the darkness with someone and say "I can't fix this for you, but I'm here for you." My passion for helping others with their own grief has become my life's work and purpose.

Becoming Comfortable with the Uncomfortable

A life-altering loss strips you down to nothing. Who you were in the world before death and tragedy took a front-row seat is no longer who you are in the aftermath. Grief and loss change everything. There is nothing untouched by it. Death and grief shape, mold, and transform who you are to your very core. When you look in the mirror after your person dies, the reflection staring back at you is often someone you don't recognize. Your personality is different after loss. Your love language(s) and needs change. Your preferences and proclivities, even how you talk, feel, think, and react, are indelibly altered. This experience changes your perspective on life, brings your priorities into focus, adjusts the people you want to spend time with, and shifts what you want from and out of life. It can also have profound effects on your spirituality and your relationship with God and religion. In essence, after the death of someone who was so integral to your life, you are forced to start over and reevaluate in many ways. You have to discover who you are, whom you want to become, what your purpose in life is now, how you interact with others around you, and how to move forward authentically in a forever-changed world without your person.

The process of discovering who you are in the wake of loss takes time. The process of learning to love the new person you are after a loss takes even longer. It takes intentionality and patience with yourself. It takes experimenting, becoming curious, and practicing getting back to life again. It is painful because you have to start imagining, dreaming, and planning for a future without your person in it. It is painful because healing and simply living again after your person dies is excruciating. But just because it is hard, doesn't mean it is wrong. In fact, I encourage doing activities that are difficult and push the boundaries within your grief. This means you're leaning into the pain instead of resisting it, and this is all part of moving through the experience. It is all part of the process of transforming yourself, building a life you love, and learning to carry your pain and loss in a manageable way. I know this isn't the life you wanted for yourself. You didn't get a choice in what happened to you but you get to decide the steps you take in the aftermath. You get to decide who you are now. It is tragic and it is beautiful, and this is the harsh dichotomy in which you must learn to live within now. You must become comfortable with living within the uncomfortable. You are now a person living with grief. You will never not be a person living with grief. It isn't fair, but it also doesn't condemn you to a bad life.

I won't sugarcoat it: learning to carry grief with more ease by creating a new life after your person's death will be one of the hardest things you've ever done, but it is worth it. You may feel like your life is over. There is so much pain to feel and mourning to be done when something beautiful comes to an end. But there is also so much magic in new beginnings. This is what starting over looks like.

1 | The Weight I Carry

My late husband, Ryan, died at the age of thirty-five from an anoxic brain injury. Ryan was randomly stung by a bee on October 14, 2021 and went into anaphylactic shock with no prior history of a bee allergy. Ryan's severe reaction caused him to go into cardiac arrest for approximately twenty minutes, resulting in a severe brain injury. We were in the prime of our lives at the time. Ryan, a K9 officer at Hatboro Police Department in Montgomery County, Pennsylvania, was just hitting his stride as a K9 officer in the community, having founded his department's first K9 unit in 2019. He was enthusiastically living out his childhood dream, training his dog, Louie, and performing patrol and drug work around the Philadelphia area. I was nearing a decade of practicing law as a medical malpractice defense attorney at a law firm in Princeton, New Jersey. Our son, Jackson, was three years old and I was twenty-six weeks pregnant with our second son at the time of Ryan's accident. Our normal, some may even say boring, figured-out lives crumbled in a matter of minutes after Ryan was stung. Ryan and I had built our lives from the ground up, having met as naïve twenty-five-year-olds, when he was a cadet in the police academy and I was in my second year of law school. We met on March 17, 2012, St. Patrick's Day, fell in love instantly, were engaged three months later, and married on October 12, 2013. We had experienced so much joy and growth as individuals, a couple, and then finally as parents in our ten years together and had planned out so much of our future. We had talked about raising our two sons and about how I would eventually move up in my firm.

Ryan would finish out his twenty years at his police department, hopefully having worked with two or three K9s, and then he wanted to retire and potentially help train dogs as a retirement gig. I would work for several more years after Ryan's retirement and then finally say goodbye to my long career in law. We talked about buying a beach house somewhere and spending our golden years together and with family, filling our days full of laughter, good company, and as Ryan would always say, "delicious food and drink." **And our entire future vanished in the time it takes to wait in line for a coffee.**

After Ryan's accident, he spent five months in hospitals and brain rehabilitation. We all prayed and hoped for a miracle that Ryan would beat all the grim odds and statistics for anoxic brain injuries, that his brain would heal and he would come home. I prayed so hard that Ryan would come back to us and that we could be a family again. But in February 2022, when Ryan was admitted for the last weeks of brain rehabilitation, repeated brain imaging revealed that the damage to Ryan's brain was beyond a miracle. Any meaningful recovery was impossible. Parts of Ryan's brain that enabled him to function had died and evaporated due to the lack of oxygen. His physician told us that there were gaping holes in the brain scan where parts of Ryan's brain should be. The parts that made him the man I fell in love with. The parts of him that made him a light in this world were gone. My mother-in-law, Karen; my sister-in-law, Morgan; and I were told by his team that Ryan would permanently be in a vegetative state, unable to know what was going on around him, interact with people, unable to eat, move any of his limbs, or have any semblance of a meaningful life. If we wanted to keep him alive in a vegetative state, there were only two options: bring him home and devote our lives to the 24/7 care that he would need and secure as much skilled nursing care that insurance would pay for, or admit him to a nursing home, where he could have lived for decades as a body in a bed, trapped in an endless Groundhog Day of nothingness. That to me felt like what Hell on Earth would be like.

Neither of these options honored who Ryan was. A man with so much life inside him, so much joy and laughter. His smile brightened an entire room, and the thought of him being kept alive and deteriorating over time, never being able to see his smile again, but just watching him suffer over and over made me sick. Every time I looked at Ryan helpless in his hospital bed all I could hear in my head was his voice scream, "Let me go!" The other options we had were palliative care and hospice. Palliative care meant Ryan living in a vegetative state and continuing him on all life-sustaining treatments and regimens, including g-tube feedings and hydration, and waiting for him to get sick or suffer a complication from his brain injury, and not treating him and allowing him to die. This option could essentially go on for years and years, with no end in sight. Waiting for something bad to happen to him while watching him struggle with copious amounts of secretions from his tracheostomy, the hyper bone growth in his limbs that caused him to grimace in pain whenever he was stretched or moved, and countless other ways in which Ryan was suffering and deteriorating from his injury, was not an option. Karen, Morgan, and I decided that hospice was really the only viable option for Ryan and for us. This meant stopping all life-sustaining measures, including Ryan's feedings and hydration, and allowing him to die, while a plethora of pain medications were administered so he wouldn't feel pain. We didn't want

Ryan to die, but dying was the only way for Ryan to be at peace. Ryan deserved peace after months of being subjected to extraordinary measures to keep him alive and being a prisoner in his own body.

Ryan was therefore admitted to hospice at his cousin Michael's house on our ten-year-anniversary of meeting, St. Patrick's Day, March 17, 2022, and he died twenty-two days later, on April 7, 2022 at the age of thirty-five. Six months of living what can only be described as Hell on Earth had come to a tragically sad ending that no one wanted. The things I saw, smelled, heard, and touched during those six months are things that will never escape my mind. The way Ryan went from a strong, healthy, handsome, capable husband and father to someone that needed his briefs changed when before he had changed his own baby's diaper, and then to a deteriorating skeleton with purple patches of death (mottling is the technical term) spread throughout his body prior to his last breath are images that no one wants to carry. This is just a small glimpse into the darkness I have learned to hold after my husband's accident and death that I have had to process repeatedly, come to some semblance of peace or acceptance with, and then have learned to carry with me as I have integrated the substantial weight of these traumatic memories into my being so they don't consume me. I have found a way to build a beautiful and meaningful life around the things that will always bear weight on my soul as I write a new chapter for myself and my two sons. It is time for you to start writing your next chapter after the death of your person as well. It is time for you to start learning who you are now in the aftermath of tragedy, tune into your needs within your grief, figure out what and who works for you in your new life, and grasp onto the joy that comes into your life after the unimaginable. Remember, you didn't have any choice in this new life, but you're making the intentional decision to start moving forward anyway. This journey will undoubtedly cause fear and uncertainty, which is only normal when we are starting over and especially when our world has been shattered by death, but I also hope you feel courageous and have faith that it won't always feel this heavy. The first load we will tackle together is the weight you carry from the physical items that are left behind when our person dies.

What to Expect in the Pages Ahead

You're about to embark on something you've likely never done before and that can be scary. As you continue reading the pages of this book, I am going to challenge you to start taking intentional, meaningful action steps into your new life without your person. I am going to give you the tools and mindset shifts you need to begin figuring out how to integrate and carry a pain that can never be extinguished or put down, but that can only be carried with you through the rest of your life. I know this may seem impossible at the moment and even thinking about creating a new life without the person you were supposed to do life with seems daunting and causes so much resistance. I completely understand and I am so sorry for your pain. But I also know that you cannot go back to the life you loved and lived before and to white knuckle a life that is no longer possible only causes more suffering. I want this book to be a soft place for you to land as you navigate the only path that is truly possible for you, forward. Turn the page once you're ready to start taking those first steps into your new life.

2 | He's Not Coming Home

We don't talk about how strange it is when our person dies and what we are left with are just their things. The items that didn't seem like they took up much space at all when our person was alive, become completely suffocating after they are gone. Our loved one's items they used in life are a constant and cruel physical reminder that there was another life in our home and now there isn't. It is often all we can see and focus on. The weight of a person's things after they die is palpable. In order for me to start writing a new chapter in my life that Ryan was not part of, I needed my physical environment to match my reality.

As I was just emerging from "fight or flight" mode in the summer following Ryan's death, I found myself completely weighed down by all of Ryan's things that surrounded me in the home we had once shared together. I hadn't touched anything while Ryan was in the hospital, up until the day that he died. I couldn't find the strength or courage to put away or organize anything in the immediate months after his death as well. Although I had known early on in Ryan's journey how sick he was and that he was likely never coming home, a part of me didn't want to give up the ghost. I was willingly in denial. Moving around and putting away his things would solidify and mean that my nightmare was real. Ryan was never coming home, and for a long while, that truth was too devastating for me to grasp. You may also find yourself grappling with realities that feel like nightmares and seem impossible to accept because they are too tragic and unfair. You may feel detached and dissociated from your body and life right now because the truth is just that unfathomable. There are some realities in life that we reject to accept with all of our being, but there comes a time where we get smacked in the face with the fact that our person is gone forever. There became a point in time for myself, a few months after Ryan died, when I looked around our home with big smiling pictures of us and all of Ryan's things taking up so much space physically, mentally, and emotionally, and it felt like torture. It felt like the smiling faces in the pictures and the things were mocking me. Perhaps you also know what I am talking about. Your happiest and most celebratory moments showcased in your home are now only a cruel reminder of the beautiful life you lived and one in which you can never live again. It is an awful thing in grief, especially in the acute, early stages that looking back on our most joyous moments becomes the most painful breeding ground for grief and what we have lost. Our home was still set up like Ryan could walk into our home at any moment and start using his things again. His sunglasses were right by our car key bowl as if he could just grab them before running out the door. All his clothes were still hanging in the closet in our bedroom. His jewelry box filled with his watches, bracelets, and police coins still sat on his bureau below drawers that were packed to the brim with his clothes and uniforms. Ryan's soap and shampoo were still in our shower, his toothbrush and toothpaste were on the sink in our bathroom, and his shoes were scattered all around the house and garage, all where he had left them. I was living in a tomb. A tomb of a beautiful life that was no longer mine to live. A tomb of broken dreams and a man that I loved so fiercely who was now dead and never coming home. I knew I could have asked someone for help with this task, but cleaning out Ryan's closet, like I had felt spreading his ashes in the sea, felt like a ritual and sacred moment that I needed to take on by myself. I knew I needed to feel every emotion that would come up and I didn't want to feel restricted, embarrassed, or stifled by anyone else's presence. It needed to just be me, Ryan's clothes, and the ghost of a man who was my husband present for these moments.

I figured that I would start with the closest in our bedroom to start cleaning out and organizing Ryan's things. Seeing all his clothes hung so neatly in our closet was perhaps one of the most painful things for me to see and they were right in my face. I swung open the doors to reveal sweatshirts, sweaters, button-down shirts, and a slew of police uniforms staring back at me. I stood in front of the closet doors taking it all in and looking at each of the items of clothing, each one signifying a memory or moment in time. A blue-and-red checkered button-down shirt caught my eye and I leaned in to see it closer. I ran my hands through the material on the sleeve and pushed the clothing surrounding it with the back of my palm so I could see the front of it. It was the shirt that Ryan had worn ten years prior on our first official date. We had gone to a Thai restaurant in Manayunk, Pennsylvania, and I had known on our first date that Ryan was my person. I don't remember what we talked about that evening, but I remember laughing a lot and genuinely enjoying each other's company. There had always been an effortlessness between us like we had known each other in our past lives and had met again in this one. I have a picture of us from that evening with Ryan in the red-and-blue checkered shirt. We looked like babies even though we were twenty-five years old, an innocence in our faces then like we didn't have a care in the world.

I snapped back to reality as I rubbed the material of Ryan's shirt between my thumb and pointer finger. *So many memories*, I thought as I looked down the row at the other pieces of hung clothing. They were just hanging lumps of fabric, but as I stood looking at all the clothing that hung so neatly in Ryan's closet that day, all I could see were birthdays, date nights, anniversaries, holidays, and special weekends together as a couple and as a family. Each piece of clothing signifying a precious memory of when Ryan was still alive. I could see his big, bright smile and hear his laugh echoing in my head as I scanned each hung item. I started to feel that familiar lump in my throat that meant tears weren't far behind. I let them fall freely as I stood in front of my dead husband's clothes. I knew if I took out every item and had a moment with each one that this experience would be excruciatingly painful, and I just wanted all his things to be sorted. I desperately needed something to feel complete, and new, like a clean slate. I needed **our** home not to feel like our home anymore because that was a lie.

You may be debating with yourself if you're ready to sort through your dead person's things. The weird and rather inconvenient thing about grief is that you're never going to feel ready to do any of these hard tasks because you will feel pain and deep, deep sorrow while you are doing them no matter if you wait five minutes or five years. Other people see lumps of fabric and items that have no meaning to them at all. You see an entire life in front of you, down to pairs of socks and underwear. Everything is a precious moment in time, a memory, a feeling with your person that is dead now. The worst part is that these memories are finite. There are no more memories to be made with your person and that truth fucking sucks. Let it just suck. You see and feel the depths and the gravity of exactly what was lost within the "things" of your person. So the thing is, you'll never feel ready and it will be painful. But if the pain of feeling like you're living in a tomb and staring at pictures of people in a life that you don't recognize anymore is more painful than doing the action of sorting through it all, then you're ready. This is exactly how I knew I was ready.

I started to grab hangers off the metal rod in the closet and throw items of clothing onto my bed, one after the other until there was a heap that looked like it may topple over. I pulled out everything in Ryan's closet including a small cabinet that contained books, training materials from work, a hefty tin of loose change, and so many other random items that Ryan had kept for safekeeping, and tossed these items on my bed. By the time I was finished emptying the closet, I was out of breath and sweating. "Jesus Christ, you have a lot of shit babe," I complained as if Ryan was in the room with me. *I am sure he is getting a kick out of this scene,* I thought to myself. Ryan had always said that I had a flair for the dramatic and he was right. This activity was no different. The sadness I had when I began this process turned to annoyance as I glared at the enormous pile of stuff I now had to go through if I wanted to sleep in my own bed that night. You may have heard of the five stages of grief: denial, anger, bargaining, depression, and acceptance. If you've lost someone precious, you're likely aware that the stages of grief don't occur in a linear fashion or in any coherent order. You don't simply make your way through the stages like a step-by-step program, move on to the next once you are finished with one stage, and are able to stop grieving and move on with life when you've reached acceptance. None of this is that simple. Life and our humanness just doesn't work that way. When you experience a life-shattering death, you certainty will feel the emotions as outlined in the traditional stages of grief. But you will likely experience them in a random and chaotic way, jumping from one to another in any given moment or on any given day. You can skip steps and go back steps. The amount of time you stay within an emotion or stage is erratic too. The five stages leave out so much of the complexity and color of the emotions one feels within the totality of the grieving experience. You will feel so many more intense emotions than just five as a griever; you will continue to emotion jump within the stages of grief and feel an array of other things as well, likely until your last breath. Your loss is yours to hold, to feel, and to navigate for the rest of your life. In a way, grief is one of the most human experiences one can have. There is no feeling or emotion left unturned. I am sure I was going through my own form of emotion jumping as I cleaned out Ryan's closest. And it was anything but a seamless, five-step process. As I stood frozen and overwhelmed trying to figure out an organized plan of attack, a blue folder that had been in the small cabinet in the closet caught my eye. I pulled it out from the heaviness of several sweatshirts and opened it slowly. Nestled in the pockets of the folder were pieces of lined paper with handwriting on it. The paper had been smoothed out but had evidence that it had once been in someone's pocket with creases and crinkles from being folded. I began reading the words on the page and I immediately recognized what it was: Ryan and my wedding ceremony. These words had been written by one of Ryan's best friends who is an Episcopalian priest, who had ironically and tragically also given Ryan his last rites before he died. I found one of the only small spaces on my bed that didn't have a huge heap of clothing covering it and sat down to read the rest of the pages in the folder. A printed page was also tucked away in the folder that Ryan had stored away. I pulled the page out gently and placed it on top of my thigh and began reading. *Our wedding vows.* I recognized them immediately and my heart sank and my stomach flipped. I was immediately transported back to the day that Ryan and I had committed our lives to one another as a married couple. To love and honor each other through sickness and health, until death do us part. Warm, fat tears dripped from my eyes onto the sheet of paper as I read our vows. It felt like I was floating outside of my body. *Surely this isn't my life. It's all just a bad dream,* I thought. The reality of it all hadn't really seeped in yet and there was still a part of me that didn't believe that Ryan was dead. It was like I had two parts of my brain at odds with one another. The rational side knew what was real. It knew what was concrete, factual, and true. But the other side of my brain just couldn't accept it because it was too far from what I could comprehend at that point in time. That part of my brain still heard Ryan's footsteps walking up the stairs in his work boots. That part of my brain still saw him or heard his voice in a crowded room. That part of my brain still expected to see his police car drive down the hill to our house and into the driveway. But all of this could not be true. The truth was that I was going through Ryan's things because he was dead and he didn't need any of his stuff anymore. The truth was Ryan was never walking up the stairs in *our home* again and all this stuff signified a life that didn't exist anymore.

Clean Slates and New Beginnings

When your person dies, you are tasked with the seemingly impossible. You have to mentally and emotionally transition from a home and a life that was "ours" to a home and a life that is just "yours." This is an extremely abrupt, painful, and messy transition to make. It is a transition that requires giving yourself the space, time, and grace to figure out how the hell you want to start rearranging and rebuilding your life from the ground up. I've been asked by countless widows and others who have lost a loved one, "When is the right time to go through their things?" and "What should I do with all their stuff?" There is no right or wrong way to complete this task and there is also no right or wrong time to make some of the transitions that we face after our person dies, including cleaning out and organizing your loved one's things, taking off your wedding rings (or deciding to wear them indefinitely), doing some redecorating, or moving to a new home or even relocating to an entirely different state or country. These two questions often provided guidance as I was making these types of decisions, "What brings me the most peace, comfort, and clarity within my grief at this moment?" and "What feels authentic and in alignment to me, my grief, and the life I am building right now?" If these questions are too complex for you to evaluate and answer in your experience of grief at the moment, then notice how your body responds to thinking about these types of tasks or starting them. I want to remind you that none of these things are ever going to be easy. You're never going to feel completely ready. These tasks will most likely come with pain and tears. But just because it is painful doesn't make it wrong.

It means that this shit is hard no matter how long you wait to do them. Healing comes from doing the difficult things, knowing it will force you to come face to face with the darkest crevices of your pain and pushing yourself to do them anyway. This is how we build confidence, strength, and a new identity after a life-altering loss. However, if just the thought of cleaning out your person's things makes you run to the bathroom to vomit and elicits a panic attack, then it isn't the right time. You need to decipher between it just being hard and painful and if the task is causing legitimate suffering. I discovered within my experience of grief that there is an important distinction between something being painful within the experience and something that causes legitimate suffering. I listen to my body to tell the difference. Does something cause me to feel like I'm going to vomit, have a panic attack, not be able to sleep, eat, or interact for an extended period of time, and be completely frozen and unable to do any activities of daily living? Then this is suffering. If something causes me to be sad, cry, and feel the very normal array of emotions within the grief experience like anger, frustration, or even guilt, I try to push myself to do these activities. This is pain, and pain is manageable. Feeling and leaning into pain is essential within the grief experience. It is how we move through it and take intentional steps forward into our new life. Only you can make that determination for yourself whether something is causing you pain or suffering. If using my metric helps you decide what you are feeling, that's great. You can always wait for a better time or ask a friend/family member or professional organizer to help you with this extremely daunting task. Ask yourself what you need and who you need to get you through this process without suffering. Pain is part of the process, but suffering can and should be avoided if possible.

If the fact that your dead loved one's things are all around your home or wearing your wedding rings is causing more pain than peace, then maybe it is time to consider making a transition. Again, there is no right or wrong here. Many people wear their wedding rings forever after the death of a spouse and some people, like myself, take them off soon after their spouse dies. For some, wearing them is a comforting connection to the person they love. For others and for myself, it reminded me of everything I had lost and of a life I couldn't live anymore. My wedding rings were contributing to my own suffering and ability to move forward because every time I looked down at them, it was like I was living a lie. I couldn't integrate my grief if I felt like I wasn't living 100 percent authentically to my own journey. Do what is right for you and your pain. Do what brings you comfort and connection. Do what makes it easier to integrate your pain and loss into your life as you move forward.

So what did I do with all of Ryan's stuff, you may be wondering? First, I made three large trunks for me and my two sons with the items that were most emblematic of Ryan, his life, our relationship, and his legacy. This included saving several of Ryan's uniforms, his police belts and vests, his favorite everyday clothes, notebooks that he wrote in, and things that truly captured who Ryan was in life. I also made each of the boys "daddy boxes" with smaller items of Ryan's including watches, bracelets, pins, photographs, sunglasses, pocket squares, police patches and coins he collected, and a small portion of Ryan's ashes in a wooden box engraved with a beautiful tree and Ryan's initials, "RJA," for Ryan Joseph Allen. I also kept fancier dress suits for each of the boys that they can hopefully wear if they choose when they are older. I wear a lot of Ryan's police and K9 t-shirts and sweatshirts in my everyday life. I also kept a forest green jacket that Ryan wore on colder days to walk Louie. That jacket makes me feel like he is wrapping his arms around me in a warm hug. I keep his police badge on my bureau that I sometimes pick up and run my fingers over the curved and grooved metal, knowing that Ryan's hands also touched it at one time and it is like we are connecting with one another in different dimensions—physically separated but spiritually intertwined through space and time forever. I keep Ryan's driver's license in my wallet with photobooth snapshots of us from a wedding. I carry Ryan and the love we shared with me always. These physical items bring me as much comfort as material objects can bring when the thing you really want is impossible—you want your person to be here with you, alive and healthy again. These items make me feel closer to Ryan. They make me feel a part of him somehow. They bring me a deep sense of peace to have and wear them. With the rest of Ryan's things that didn't feel necessary to keep and store, I asked family and friends to take items that gave them peace and comfort in their own grief after Ryan's death. I threw away his shoes and other items that no one wanted and I donated the rest. In sum, I kept and stored the special, cherished, and symbolic items. The things that truly embodied Ryan and reminded me of him. The things that would help our sons get to know how amazingly loving, funny, and heroic their daddy was. I let the important people in our lives take things that were duplicative but were also very much "Ryan" and I threw away or donated the rest. I personally knew that this project would be arduous and emotionally draining so I asked for help for the things beyond Ryan's closet. I hired professional organizers to assist in organizing, storing, and getting rid of the rest of his items to take some of the heavy load off this task for me. If you're able to hire professional help as well, it is a true blessing and was so helpful in this process. If this isn't a reasonable option for you, and if you're ready, ask for help from family or friends. Transfer some of the heavy load of grief to others when you can, even if it is only for a short while. You need some relief. This goes for going through a loved one's personal items but also in so many other aspects of grief. Don't think you have to do it all on your own.

Another important thing I did during the same time period as I was going through Ryan's things after he died was do some simple redecorating. It felt very cathartic for me to create a space for me and my sons that felt like our home and not necessarily the same home that I had created with Ryan. I needed my environment to be a physical reminder that life was different, that I was different, and that this life was new. I needed to breathe new life into my space. So I did easy things that made a huge difference. Give yourself permission to experiment and explore what big or small changes within your own physical environment support you in your own grief. Is it selling your couch that is ten years old and getting a new one to make your living room feel completely different? Is it turning your basement into an at-home gym so you can work out in the comfort of your own home? Is it simply just new decorative pillows on your bed? Nothing is wrong or off-limits. Do what makes you feel just a little bit lighter within the heaviness of life after loss. A reminder here that making no changes at all is also an intentional and important decision. If leaving everything as is for the time being feels right to you, then that is your answer. You can always reassess down the road. Again, do what brings some peace and ease to your tumultuous heart. What made me feel just a little bit lighter within my own grief? I took down the big photographs of me and Ryan that made me feel like a knife was stabbing me in the heart every time I looked at them and replaced them with art I love and photographs of my life after Ryan died. I put up art and photographs and that made me feel calm, and centered, and that brought me joy in my home. The photographs I placed of Ryan around the house were placed strategically so it felt like we were honoring and memorializing him versus that he was living in the home. These changes made the most sense to my grieving brain and my tender heart. These changes felt like they reflected my new reality and the life I was trying to build around my loss. I specifically made certain my bedroom felt like mine and not mine and Ryan's by purchasing a new lamp and a new duvet, both white in color. A fresh start, a clean slate, a new beginning. What I didn't know at the time I was making small aesthetic changes to the home I shared with Ryan was that bigger and more drastic changes to my life would be just on the horizon. Life after the death of your person is beautiful and unpredictable in that way. As you are working on yourself and processing your grief and trauma, life can bring people and opportunities into your life that you didn't expect or see coming and they change everything, just like how meeting Ryan changed the entire trajectory of my life in 2012. My second chapter of life without Ryan was no different.

Almost fifteen months after Ryan died, I sold the house that was supposed to be our forever home, the place where we planned on raising our family together. I would be remiss to not talk about this very significant transition in my own grief journey. The decision to move from the home I shared with Ryan was a difficult one. There were so many parts of that home that felt so much like Ryan, that reminded me of the beautiful life we had built together. But it also reminded me so much of how much was lost after Ryan's accident and how the life we planned together would never come to fruition. Our home was also the place where Ryan went into anaphylaxis from a bee sting, where I had to give him CPR on our front porch, and where he went into cardiac arrest. As much as I tried to separate these traumatic memories from the physical locations where they took place, I found that trauma is very powerful. I couldn't walk into my front door without somewhat reliving the worst day of my life in my mind. Even though I didn't let these triggers take over my life, I found that the home I shared with Ryan was a landmine for both beautiful and incredibly painful memories of life in the "before," life before Ryan's accident.

Living in a home that felt so much like Ryan and reminded me so much of our life together became increasingly painful when I met Anthony in the summer after Ryan died. By the winter that followed, Anthony and I began talking about a future together as a family, and I found it difficult to imagine building a new life and forging a new identity in the home that Ryan and I had stamped our "forever home." Living there didn't make me feel closer to Ryan, but rather it exacerbated the heaviness of what I had lost and could never get back. It was like living in a house of broken dreams. Anthony additionally felt it was important to begin and build our lives together as a couple in a physical environment that had no history, emotional charge, or triggers attached. I agreed that moving felt like the decision that was the most authentic and in alignment with the life I was trying to establish after Ryan's death. The home that Anthony, my two sons, and I moved into on 23 June 2023 was our fresh start and it has been one of the most healing decisions I've made since Ryan's accident. Maybe you have also taken a leap of faith in your new life after loss that has allowed you a pocket of peace in the vast darkness that death creates in its wake. I want to commend you for taking a chance on yourself and your new life. Taking any step forward after the unimaginable loss that you've experienced is evidence that you maintain hope, perhaps even without any evidence right now, of finding the light again. Remember that no step or leap is too trivial.

When You're Ready

Making a big transition, like moving, after your person's death is a big deal. Like all the choices I made in the wake of Ryan's death, they were what made the most sense to me and the life I was creating. Some of the decisions I made may not make sense to you and your own grief journey or life at the moment. You may feel incredibly connected to your loved one by living in the house you shared together. It may bring you great peace to be in the physical space you once shared with the person you love. Moving may also not be a feasible option for you at the moment even if it is something you want to do. The bottom line is always do what is right for you, at the time it is right for you. Do what brings you peace knowing that as you change in the future, your grief will feel different too, and therefore your needs and wants will inevitably shift. New possibilities that you may have never considered earlier in your grief because they just didn't feel right may seem like new opportunities now or they may in the future.

- **Allow yourself to change your mind. Allow yourself to be flexible and open to the endless possibilities that life has to offer for you.** Grief often makes us feel like we are in a tiny box that we can't escape. It can feel like grief limits our potential and our choices in life, but it can actually expand our potential and choices if we allow it to. Simply shifting your focus from feeling stuck to being curious about what life has to offer can be a powerful tool.

- **If it helps, write down the things you may be curious about in your life now after your loss.** Does a new career sound interesting? Do you feel butterflies in your stomach when you think about dating again? Do you get excited visualizing yourself driving a new car or even with a new haircut? Write down the things you are curious about and analyze how each of these options makes you feel. Note the emotions that each of these possibilities elicit next to the things you are curious about. If some of the possibilities you write down bring excitement and more curiosity as you allow your mind to visualize yourself experiencing these new things, those are the opportunities you should explore more. If you're feeling like you're trapped in a box made of walls of grief, this is your permission to get curious and explore the possibilities.

- **Don't compare your grief experience with anyone else's.** It is so crucial to remember that your loss and your experience of grief is yours and yours alone. You will inevitably meet others in real life or see others online who have suffered loss, even the same type of loss as you, and they are grieving and deciding to move forward differently than what feels authentic to you. That's OK. When you get caught up in what other grievers are doing, you can easily feel like you are doing grief wrong, that you aren't moving at the right pace, or that the transition(s) you are making or want to make in your life after a loss are incorrect because they are different from someone else's. This can cause so much unnecessary shame and guilt. So please remember this. You cannot do grief wrong. This experience is messy to be sure, but you cannot mess this up. Do what feels right and authentic to you, in the time that feels right to you, and drown out the noise.

- **Be kind, gentle, and patient with yourself.** This is something I wish I had practiced more when I was attempting to put the pieces of my life back together after my entire world shattered after Ryan's medical event. I wouldn't have been so hard on myself on the days that felt heavier. I would have given myself more grace and compassion during a time when I needed it the most. Remember how powerful your inner dialog is and be cognizant of the things you tell yourself. You are capable and brave and none of this is easy.

- **A summary of more practical advice when it comes to what to do with your loved one's things.** This may ease your tender heart when it comes to what to do with your person's things, but it also may be hard to hear. It isn't realistic to keep everything. A good rule of thumb is to keep and store special, cherished, and symbolic items of your person. The items that bring you peace, joy, or are nostalgic. For items that are old or that will never be used again, like shoes, it is perfectly OK to throw these things out when you're ready. If it feels good to you, allow other people you love and trust the opportunity to take some items, like clothing, that you do not want or need. If an item (big or small) doesn't make sense in the new life you're creating after loss, it is perfectly fine to donate these items or sell them. You also don't have to figure out what to do with everything all at once. Do things at your own pace, and if possible hire someone to help you with this process or ask a friend or family member to help if you're feeling overwhelmed by this task.

Be aware that when you start taking intentional action into your new life after loss, you'll start to feel resistance. Some of this resistance will be internal, while some of it will come from external forces, including friends, family members, colleagues, strangers, and society at large that may not understand what it is like to move through this experience. Some may show discomfort or even exhibit blatant disgust or outrage that you are intentionally trying to find joy and purpose again in a life that you never asked for. You'll find that as you start to put back the pieces of your life after loss, many won't cheer you on. In fact, you may be condemned for not adhering to antiquated societal standards of what a mourning person should look and act like. Let them misunderstand you. If they are in a position to judge and condemn, then they are lucky enough to not understand. It is painful when you have suffered and it seems that people you know and society expects you to suffer more. You can be pissed and hurt that this is the way of the world but don't let them steal your well-earned joy like I almost did. Learn from my own experience that I'm about to share.

3

Don't Let Them Steal Your Joy

As a young widow at the age of thirty-five with a toddler and a baby, I was not immune to people thinking I was doing grief "wrong" because it didn't fit with their narrative. I promised myself after Ryan died that I would live life for both of us, which meant living on my own terms and in a way that made me feel content and fulfilled. But I soon discovered on my quest of living authentically as a young widow that people hated me for finding some semblance of happiness in the aftermath of tragedy.

I was startled awake from a deep sleep when I realized that the repetitive sound that I was hearing in my dream was actually my alarm going off. Without opening my eyes, my head still snuggled into my pillow, and wet drool still glistening on my cheek. I stretched my left arm out to reach my phone on the nightstand and attempted to hit the snooze button. Instead, I swiftly knocked my phone and it rocketed to the floor with a obnoxiously loud *thump*. "Fuck," I muttered into the pillow as I shifted my body to the edge of the bed and swung my arm back and forth on the carpet, trying to find my phone and stop the incessant ringing. Exasperated that I had abruptly been disturbed from a rare restful sleep, I picked up my phone and tapped hard and repeatedly with my pointer finger on the alarm button. Finally, some silence. Then as on cue, I heard baby Leo on the monitor starting to rustle around in his crib and whine quietly. Surely he would be in a full-on cry in no time, so I decided to mindlessly scroll Instagram before willing myself out of my warm and cozy bed to get Leo before he started to wail.

I clicked on the Instagram app and I was immediately bombarded with the tiny red notifications letting me know I had new likes, followers, and comments. I clicked on activity and started to read through some of the comments on my most recent vulnerable post about finding love again after Ryan's death, which had occurred six months earlier. My heart started thumping in my chest as I remembered that I had posted last night and then had immediately put away my phone, a little unsure and nervous about the response. It felt like I was holding my breath as I started to scroll and read. "Wait a minute. You already 'fell in love' again? Really? To me, that doesn't sound like you really truly loved your husband. How disrespectful of his memory." Another commenter wrote, "The baby probably isn't your husband's since you were obviously messing around with your boyfriend before your husband died. No one falls in love that fast after their spouse dies [surprise face emoji]." I suddenly felt the heat of anger rise from my belly and rush to my throat. "What the fuck?" I said into my phone screen as I flung away my comforter with my free hand and climbed out of bed. I couldn't read another word. I swiped up on my screen to exit the Instagram app. The warmness that had rushed to my throat suddenly formed into a lump and I felt tears welling in the corner of my eyes. *How could people be so cruel? Why did these people want me to suffer more? Why is it a bad thing that I have found some semblance of happiness again? They just don't understand what I've been through. What I've lost and fought so hard to find again.* These thoughts swirled around my head as I started to scuffle out of my bedroom to the hallway where Leo's high-pitched crying echoed.

The Weight of Opinions

When I decided to share about my new relationship after Ryan's death on social media, I knew there would be people that would be critical. What I didn't expect or what I honestly didn't comprehend is how vicious people can be behind their anonymous screens. Since the first time I shared my experience of dating and unexpectedly finding an amazing man that I wanted to start building a new life with after Ryan died, I've received hundreds, if not thousands, of encouraging messages from strangers and acquaintances on social media. And I've also received dozens of the most hateful messages someone could imagine. I've been called an adulterous, a bad wife, and a bad mom for letting someone new into my children's lives so soon. I've been called selfish and co-dependent for needing a man in my life and told that I should try to be alone for the "right" amount of time and just focus on my children to give myself a proper mourning period before even starting to think about dating again. Each message signifying that society knows me and my grief better than I know myself and my own grief. Each message assuming that there is a rule and etiquette book for being a young widow with children. Each message screaming to me that I was doing grief "wrong." I read somewhere once that as humans we can be surrounded by positive, but if one bad thing happens we will put all of our time and energy into focusing on the negative. As humans, we obsess about the minuscule negative in our lives in a sea full of positives. That was true for me when it came to those vile online messages. For a short time after I started sharing my love-after-loss experience, I let the few disgusting and ignorant words of complete strangers on the internet make me feel defensive and like I had done something wrong by falling in love while I was a newly grieving widow.

I was fortunate that Karen and Morgan were kind, loving, and understanding through the experience. As much as I knew I wasn't doing anything wrong and I was being authentic to myself by opening up my heart again, I also knew that this was extremely painful for Karen and Morgan. My new relationship was just another harsh reminder that Ryan was dead. It opened up complex questions and worries about their places in my, Jackson's, and Leo's lives with another man and another man's family in the picture. I was fully aware of the weight that being in a relationship with Anthony would cause and I tried my best to approach the situation with as much care and compassion as I could, as we all navigated this complicated terrain of melding families after death. I led in the only way that would honor my deep love and admiration for both of them, which was with my whole heart and with transparency. I shared with Morgan when I started dating to spare Karen any additional pain for no reason, and shared with both Karen and Morgan when me and Anthony became serious and they both met him separately when the time was right for them. Since that time, Karen and Morgan have been extremely gracious and welcoming to both Anthony and his family, inviting them to special events and celebrations. Obviously, there is always that ever-present elephant in the room, which is that a very special and amazing man is dead and that's why we are all in this situation. That elephant took up the entire room in the beginning, but it has slowly started to shrink and fade into the background as all the families have gotten to know each other better and have warmed to the idea of integrating families and all the emotions involved. Karen has even continued to come to Anthony and my new home to spend time with the boys and help us with dinner and bedtime, which she has done every single week without fail since Ryan died in April 2022. Experiencing life with my children, Ryan's family, and now Anthony's family is incredibly beautiful to experience, although inevitably messy and emotional at times. The boys and I have one more family to love us fiercely and they do it with so much ease. Ryan's family is also an ever-present and extremely important part of our lives and I am so grateful for that. None of this has been easy, but we are all moving forward and giving everyone grace knowing there is no guidebook for any of this.

One slow Sunday morning as the first summer without Ryan slowly faded into the fall, I stood in the kitchen looking out the window and sipping iced coffee out of a Mason jar. Anthony was making pancakes for me and the boys, Jackson was playing with his Legos and watching *Bluey* in the living room, and baby Leo was laughing and cooing in his high chair waiting eagerly to be fed as he sipped his milk out of his bottle. Anthony and I had only been together for a few months during which time I focused on my healing journey, pouring into my mental, physical, and emotional health like it was my lifeline. My budding relationship with Anthony was being experienced in parallel with the activities I was doing to help myself out of the darkness and hopelessness I felt in the aftermath of Ryan's death. It was just the start of my journey, but I started to feel an initial shift in my overall energy and well-being. I was used to always feeling on the verge of tears, or like I wanted to rage out, and my anxiety was so high that I couldn't think straight or be in the moment. I was slowly recovering from being in survival mode and it was hard for me to feel at ease, safe, and secure. But that morning, I felt happy. For the first time in a while, I realized that somewhere between complete despair and trying to find some peace and normalcy in the aftermath of Ryan's death, I had stumbled upon my first glimpse at contentment. The beautiful thing about contentment is that it feels like the perfect combination of joy and solace, two things that disappear instantly when someone you love dies. This is why when you feel your first inkling of contentment, it is so important to pause, take it in, and surrender to it so you can start collecting evidence that **life can be good again**. I was still grieving; of course, I would always be grieving in some capacity, but the heaviness that once felt pressed so firmly on my chest showed evidence that morning that it could lift, if only fleetingly at first. But now I knew it was possible for me. It felt like relief, hope, and like I was living again for the first time in so long.

That morning I made a promise to myself that no matter what criticism I may receive in the future for living authentically after the death of my husband, I wouldn't let it deter me from holding onto every glimmer of hope and magic that I had created from complete wreckage and darkness. I had been through a war after Ryan's accident and experienced things that will forever haunt me. Through it all, I had somehow maintained faith that life wouldn't always feel so heavy, even when it felt like it was crushing and suffocating me. There was no way in hell that I was going to let strangers on the internet or even family or friends make me feel like I needed to fit their mold of what a young, grieving widow should look like and delay or repress my own happiness. I had earned every ounce of joy that I had been able to conjure again after my world fell apart, and I wouldn't let anyone take that away from me.

In the background of creating a new life and identity after a life-altering loss are other people's opinions and criticisms. You'll find when you start making some transitions and decisions after the death of your person, like pursuing a new career, starting to date, moving, or countless other changes that you can make after someone dies, that the opinions and criticisms from others including family, friends, colleagues, and strangers will inevitably start flooding in. I was fortunate that when I decided to leave the practice of law and go all in to pursue a new career helping others as a grief coach, that the people closest to me didn't share any of their skepticism, at least not to my face. There were of course strangers online that said that I was not qualified to support others through grief because I am not a licensed therapist or counselor. However, many of my clients start working with me after traditional therapists and counselors can't help them because these professionals cannot fully relate to a loss they have not experienced. A life-altering loss can only be truly understood by someone who has walked the same hellish path. Unfortunately, I can relate to how a death rearranges someone's world on an intimate level, in a way that others who have not gone through a similar experience cannot.

When you do begin making changes after the death of your person, some of the people in your life may suggest not making any "big" changes or decisions for a year or two. And if you don't feel comfortable making any big decisions for that long or even longer, that's OK. However, for those who are called to take leaps of faith or make some changes in their lives because it feels right to do so, I want you to know that there isn't some kind of magical clarity that happens after a year or even two years after your world falls apart. Your willingness, your capacity, your ability, your excitement, and your curiosity to explore what the world looks like and feels like for you without your person can happen at any time after their death. There is no timetable. There is no socially acceptable time period to start making life decisions for yourself after a loved one dies. You do not need to wait for permission to reach for joy, purpose, or love again. When your person dies, nothing in your world makes sense anymore. Many times going back to life as you knew it before your person's death feels wrong. This is because going through trauma and having endured the death of your person upends and adjusts everything you thought you knew about life and yourself. You are not the same person you once were. The world as you know it is indelibly changed, shifted, and transformed. After Ryan died, there were both big and little decisions to be made, each symbolizing a building block of how I was intentionally choosing to move forward with my life.

When you let other people and society dictate when the "right" time is to start evolving, transforming, and growing in your life within grief, you are delaying and repressing your own authenticity and your own happiness.

I want to wrap up this section by reminding you that you're a fucking adult even after your world falls apart. You are still able to make rational, grown-up decisions. If you endured traumas like I have, you likely had to make hundreds, if not thousands of huge decisions, including life-and-death decisions. You may feel lost right now, but you are capable. Many people will recommend keeping things "status quo" and most of these people in your life mean well. They are trying to be helpful. But the truth is, they are not living within your grief day in and day out. What may have seemed like sage, rational advice in your world before loss, may not be what you need or crave as you live and survive after a life-altering loss. You know what is best for you. You know whether changes and life transitions are necessary within your grief and you know what to keep the same. Capturing and holding onto feelings of living again is healing. It is survival. Don't let anyone take that away from you.

The Things We Do to Survive

I could feel my heart starting to beat harder and harder in my chest as baby Leo began to whine in his carrier. It was a quarter to six in the evening, and I had just gotten home from picking up my four-year-old, Jackson, at daycare with Leo, who was four months old. It was the end of May, almost two months after Ryan's death. It was also the start of witching hour in our home. I dreaded this time of day the most because it was always so chaotic, and unpredictable, and when I was prone to becoming overstimulated by too much noise and action happening all around me. Jackson threw his shoes, coat, and book bag on the floor of the playroom and ran through the kitchen, as I hurried to unbuckle Leo in his carrier before his whines transitioned to a full-blown wail. Leo's cries were particularly triggering to me in the early days after Ryan died. "Jackson! Please come in here and pick up your things!" I yelled into the air. I heard his little feet in socks pitter-patter on the hardwood floor in my direction. He stopped in front of me as I scooped Leo up and started patting his back to soothe him.

"Mama, I am hungry and tired," Jackson whined as he started to pick up his things off the floor. My grieving heart and mind craved quiet, stillness, and rest when my world with two small boys demanded so much of me that I didn't possess. At the end of the day, I felt like I was running on fumes and I gave my boys all that I had left in me. In all honesty, in those early days of grief and navigating solo parenting, what I had left in me wasn't very much.

I placed Leo in his high chair and looked in the fridge to figure out what to heat up for Jackson's dinner. Leo started to cry almost immediately. "Mama! I'm hungry!" Jackson whined again as he tugged on my shirt. I couldn't even hear myself think over Leo's cries. I again noticed my heart beating faster, faster, faster in my chest. I shut my eyes and took a few deep breaths to calm myself before speaking, but I felt the warm wrath of anger bellowing up from my belly into my throat. I tried my damndest to keep my composure before I started to speak to avoid completely losing my shit on my four-year-old. "Jackson, I am trying to get dinner together for you. Can you please sit in the living room and wait a few minutes? There is only one of me," I pleaded with him. And in that statement, there it was. That terrible, awful truth again. It was just me and my sons. Ryan was dead. He wasn't here to share any of the physical, mental, and emotional load of parenting with me. There was no one else fully responsible for these two little people. There wasn't anyone else to pick up Leo and soothe him. There wasn't anyone else to make dinner for the boys or put them to bed. I wanted to be a mother, but I hadn't made the decision to be a mother like this, without the person I wanted to parent with. It was just me and that reality hadn't truly hit me yet.

Jackson shuffled away with a frown on his face in defeat as Leo's cries grew louder and louder. I stared into the refrigerator but I was so overly stimulated that my brain couldn't process what was right in front of my eyes. I felt like I was going to crawl out of my skin and scream, but instead, I quickly removed the tray off of Leo's high chair and plucked him up, placing his chubby little body over my left shoulder and patting his back again. "It's okay ... it's okay ... it's okay," I repeated over and over to him but also to myself. *I need a drink*, I thought. I turned swiftly and started to shuffle with Leo in my arms, through the kitchen and then through the playroom, and finally to the door to the garage, where I knew there were Blue Moons in the refrigerator. I swung open the door to the garage and stepped toward the refrigerator which was just a couple of paces from the door. I opened the right side of the fridge, grabbed the first brown bottle with the familiar Blue Moon label that I spotted, went back inside, and walked back into the kitchen with Leo still in my arms. I found myself in front of the white marble countertop and I twisted off the bottle cap and took a few big gulps. I slowly pulled the bottle away from my lips and took a deep breath. My breath and heart started to slow ever so slightly as I swayed back and forth with Leo. I took another few sips before setting the beer bottle down on the countertop and returning to the fridge to figure out what to heat up for dinner.

In crisis and trauma, we all resort to coping mechanisms or self-medication in order to survive. It is what we do as humans when our world has fallen apart. Some turn to alcohol. Some turn to food or shopping. Some turn to excessive cleaning (I know this because when I was pregnant and couldn't drink, this is what I did). In essence, we create a bubble of control in a space that no longer has any order or control. We don't feel safe or comfortable in our lives anymore because we realize just how quickly and easily the people that we love can be ripped away from us without warning. So we escape, distract, and divert our attention away from the pure agony that we feel from losing someone we love in a new world that feels completely foreign and unsafe. We don't want to feel the enormous weight and how terrible that reality truly is, so we do anything to numb ourselves to just get through the next unbearably painful and long moment. We are humans and therefore we avoid pain and seek pleasure at all costs. It is what we do. It is biological and predictable in fact. After my husband died, I used alcohol as a way to smooth the darkest and tumultuous edges of my life that felt like it was swirling out of control. I used alcohol during bedtime so I could parent a baby and a toddler without losing my ever-loving mind. I used alcohol to dull the intense anxiety, fear, and pain that comes after you lose your person. Even if just for a short while, it gave me a sense of "everything is OK," even though it wasn't.

I am not going to condone drinking as a way to deal with grief or say that this habit was healthy and/or productive. But for a time period, having a drink or two each night during dinner and bedtime became my widow ritual I so desperately needed to take the edge off of my grief and posttraumatic stress disorder (PTSD) symptoms. In a period of six months between October 2021 and April 2022, I had endured more trauma than most people experience in an entire lifetime, one trauma after the other. It began with watching my husband go into anaphylactic shock in front of me and having to give him CPR on our front porch, to witnessing him wither away from the handsome, strong man he once was, to nothing but a shell of his former self, skin suctioned to bones before taking his last breath. He was only thirty-five years old when he died. And I was only thirty-five years old, and our babies were four years old and four months old. There are things that no one should have to endure while they are here on Earth, and an unnatural, traumatic death of someone you wanted to spend your life with in the prime of life is on that list. And so I am left with so much that is irreconcilable to my brain and heart. There are images, smells, and sounds that are burned into the fiber of my soul that I will have to carry for decades. They are the images, smells, and sounds of sickness, death, and of a broken future. So when my husband died, I drank to make these horrors a little less hellish to carry inside of me as I fiercely tried to grab onto the light and living again. Drinking as a coping mechanism for the symptoms, like overstimulation, that flowed from my grief after my husband died, was something I talked about and worked through with my own grief therapist. By the time I started mentoring grief coaching clients at the end of January 2023, the majority of the time, I didn't need that crutch to manage the intensity of my emotions. However, all of the horrors I experienced are still with me. It is impossible to erase my memory of them. It is impossible for my body and spirit to forget. I still get overstimulated by my children and certain life activities at times. But unlike before, because of my own work in therapy, through my training to become a certified grief coach, and my own life experience of trial and error, I am able to implement the tools and strategies I have adopted so I can move through these very uncomfortable times with more ease and grace. I remind myself daily that I am only human, carrying so much darkness, so I give myself so much grace for going through what I did and still being able to stand. **Give yourself credit for going through the unimaginable and surviving too. You are here and that is everything.** I am far from perfect and I will never be done healing. But my grief does not consume me like it once did. The pain lives inside of me; I have just become so much better with carrying it. It may be hard to imagine a life where grief doesn't feel all consuming, but let me be evidence that although it takes work, time, and practice to achieve, that you can learn to hold and carry what is weighing you down like I did. Additionally, give yourself so much love and understanding for what you've lived through, none of this is easy.

I felt guilty for a while for the things I had to do in order to survive my hardest days. I felt guilty for needing a drink to get through bedtime with my children. I would think to myself, *what kind of mother needs a drink to get dinner on the table and get her kids to bed?* I have discovered, on the other side of the most acute and painful season after my husband's death, that I was a mother who was doing her very best to function and take care of her children through a seemingly impossible situation, one that was not of my own making or choice. There is so much of this time period that was messy and nonoptimal that I would like to shed light on because perhaps you are in the trenches of grief and need some reassurance that it isn't just you that feels like they don't have their shit together. Aside from the drinking, during this time I did so many things to just get through the day. I didn't step foot inside a grocery store and I didn't cook for well over a year after Ryan died. Any food that we consumed was delivered right to our door and my children survived for a while on premade meals, mac 'n' cheese, and chicken nuggets. In my old life, although I didn't love cooking, I planned, purchased the ingredients for, and prepared most meals in our home because being a first responder's wife demanded that of me. I enjoyed having dinner on the table when Ryan got home from his shifts at work and it was something he appreciated. After he died, thinking about doing all the steps that are involved with preparing a home-cooked meal was overwhelming, sometimes even bringing me to tears to think about everything that was involved comparatively with how little I could muster to do.

I had very little capacity for the chores that I had done effortlessly in my past life before loss. In my past life, I had been a busy trial attorney, juggling working full-time, helping to run a household, and being a wife and mother. I ran on all cylinders day in and day out without any issues. But grief and trauma had completely altered my baseline for doing life because all of my energy, in the beginning, was being surrendered to my grief. While my children ate microwaved dinners, I survived on coffee, vodka sodas, Blue Moons, protein bars, and small meals like oatmeal or eggs because that was all I could stomach in those early days. Living in fight or flight mode all day long for months on end had wreaked havoc on my entire system. It destroyed my appetite and it took me a very long time to feel the desire to eat again, so I could start focusing on nutrition in order to regain the strength I had lost in crisis. Additionally, everyday tasks like putting a load of laundry in the wash, folding it, and putting it away took me a week to accomplish, usually just in time to start another full load. I could only make one or two important phone calls a day because they were incredibly draining and I found myself needing to lie down after them. Jackson ate all of his meals in front of the TV so I could manage baby Leo's relentless physical demands as a fresh baby. Jackson had to learn to be way more independent since the age of three and a half than I would like to admit. He has been forced to grow up so much faster than his peers since his daddy's accident. He experienced and had to do things that other kids his age have never had to do. Again and like a broken record, I did the best I could under the circumstances. Although none of my life in the aftermath of Ryan's death would be considered picture-perfect, my boys were loved and taken care of. But I simply could not be the kind of person and mother I had been before my husband's accident and death. I needed to give myself more grace and patience.

The things we do or the way we act in the depths of grief in order to survive aren't wrong or right, they just are because they have to be. I did the best I possibly could with the reality that I had been given. Perhaps you find yourself feeling guilty because you cannot be the person or mother or both that you were before your world fell apart. You may feel guilty that all you have the energy for is to sit with your kids and watch TV on the couch instead of going to the park like you used to. You may feel guilty that you microwaved mac 'n' cheese for the fourth time this week because your brain is so full and your body is so weary that you can't even bring yourself to go on your computer to do an online grocery order. You may need alcohol to ease your anxious and overstimulated heart and mind. You may be wearing the same pajamas for three days and haven't had the energy to shower because the person you love is dead and nothing seems to matter, especially looking put together. You may have snapped at a complete stranger on the phone because they innocently asked to speak to your husband and you had to explain for the thousandth time that your husband cannot come to the phone because he is dead. You are exhausted to your bones. You are feeling the heaviest and most defeated you have ever felt. You're scared and lonely and the only person that could ease your fears isn't here. You desperately want to be productive and just start moving but you're cemented to where you lay, sit, or stand. And I want you to know that this is all grief because this was me. It is normal to feel this way. It is also normal to feel guilty that you're not the person you once were and that you have limited bandwidth for everyday life.

Grief and trauma change everything in your world and now is not the time to force what cannot be forced. From experience, this will only lead to more suffering and more guilt. I want you to do the best you can with the shitty hand you've been thrown and I want you to change and manage your expectations of yourself for this season, knowing that it will not last forever. A season is just that, a time period that always transitions and evolves. We are not intended to bloom in every season and this is especially true within grief. Yet, this time period of grief is necessary, although exquisitely painful and frustrating. You will be indelibly altered through this experience as you work your way out of the quicksand that is the most acute phase after losing your person. Do what you can, knowing that what you are doing is everything you have to give at the moment. And if you have children, lead with love and compassion for yourself and your babies. Most importantly, forgive yourself for the things you had to do in order to survive your worst days. I have learned that the only person you absolutely need to forgive after the death of your person in order to move forward and build a beautiful life is yourself. I have found this to be a non-negotiable.

The Weight of the Unforgivable

You don't necessarily have to let go of the wrongdoings that happened to you to still find solace within your life after loss. You do not need to forgive the people who didn't throw you a life raft when you were underwater and drowning. There are events that transpired while I was going through the worst days of my life that I can't write or talk in detail about because I am protecting things that are important to me. They were cruel, harsh, shocking, and unnecessary. I am certain some of you reading this have also endured certain injustices having gone through crises or trauma that you cannot talk about because you are protecting something or someone as well. Maybe one day when the time is right I will write about these things for the world, but for now, they are just for me and a few other individuals to know. Needless to say, after Ryan died, I was left to face the unfair events that had taken place, and the people that caused them, and I was full of rage and hurt by how poorly certain things were handled when I was at my most wounded and vulnerable. Unfortunately, my vulnerability and weakness while my world was falling apart were exploited by selfish people who didn't treat my tragedy with the care it deserved, but rather as a cruel business transaction. All humanity and truth were left out of the equation. I knew in the early aftermath of Ryan's death that I either had to forgive the people who had caused me harm or come to peace with the fact that I didn't have to forgive these people or what happened, while still being able to move forward without anger in my heart. I chose the latter. I have found acceptance that there are things in life that happen that are so unforgivable and merciless that I should be under no obligation to give these individuals grace or absolution. What I have done is I've given myself grace by not feeling the pressure or need to have to excuse the inexcusable behavior of others in the name of "finding peace." I haven't forgiven, I will never forget, and yet I still have been able to take steps forward without the rage and hurt that I once held within me from the events that happened.

You also have to take inventory of the events that occurred and the people that caused them as a result of your loss that fill you with anger. You have to ask yourself this important question: "Do I have to forgive in order to move forward without anger in my heart or can I come to peace without forgiving the inexcusable and move forward with solace knowing it is my choice if I decide not to forgive?" The choice is yours and yours alone. Only you can know what is right for you and your grief. Only you can know what you're able to hold and carry with you through life and what you need to release in order to live a beautiful life after the death of your person. If you have to, make a list of the people and wrongdoings that you have to choose to forgive or not in order to take the necessary steps forward. Decide whether it is possible for you to carry each without forgiveness but with acceptance of that non-forgiveness. You'll find that there are some things that you'll need to forgive and release to move forward and others that you'll want to carry. As with everything in grief, there is no wrong or right. There is just "is" and what is authentic to you and your grief. Continue to carry anything you need to hold onto with a newfound reconciliation and release what you need to. You'll need this space when you discover within the experience of grief that the early support you receive after your person dies will fade, if not abruptly then slowly and surely in the months following the funeral or memorial. You can't control any of this, but you can control the relationship you build with yourself after loss and learn to become comfortable with being your own safe haven, source of comfort, and sounding board. I'll show you how this is possible and how to navigate life when the grief lasagnas stop being delivered to your doorstep and what you're left with is your grief on a silver platter.

Some Affirmations

- I didn't choose this life, but I get to control what happens next.
- It isn't my responsibility to sacrifice my own comfort in grief and life, for other people's comfort.
- I am not responsible for other people's grief and healing.
- I do not owe anyone an explanation or reasoning for how I choose to move forward. They don't have to agree or even understand, but if they want to be in my life, they must be respectful and kind.
- Everyone doesn't deserve to know the details of my life and my story. Just because someone asks doesn't mean I have to share. Not everyone gets a front-row seat to my tragedy.
- Just because there may be judgment or criticism doesn't mean what I'm doing is wrong. It simply means that I need to do what's best for me despite what others think. No one else is living my life.

- What people think about me is none of my business, it's theirs.
- The boundaries I choose to create in my life and my grief aren't aggressive or unkind. They are protecting my peace and someone's negative reaction to the boundary doesn't mean it isn't necessary or what I need.
- My grief is my responsibility, no one else's.

4 | When the Grief Lasagnas Stop Coming

A couple weeks had passed since Ryan's accident and I was settling into my daily routine as an exhausted, overwhelmed, and pregnant caretaker for my husband. Life now consisted of the following: waking up before the sun on little to no sleep; dragging myself out of bed so I could do the only thing that I had any control over, which was doing my hair and makeup so I didn't look like a complete wreck; dropping my three-year-old off at daycare; driving more than an hour to the hospital and making sure I was there in time for the doctor's morning rounds on Ryan; staying until I couldn't stay any longer without being late to pick up Jackson from daycare; driving more than an hour home; getting Jackson ready for bed; and passing out on his bed, which usually happened while I was fully dressed and with makeup on. This special type of hell was on rinse and repeat.

It was a little past six in the evening when I pulled up in front of our home in my BMW. There was only a soft pink and orange glow left in the setting sky and I thought how odd it was that something so beautiful could exist in the same world where my life felt so ugly and messy. It was strange that as Ryan was fighting for his life in the neuro ICU and my life was escaping rapidly through my fingers like sand, there was still normal, happy, life happening around us. The sun still rose each morning and it set each night marking the passage of time while I was in a hellish limbo. I was frozen in my seat staring at the white garage door that was illuminated by the headlights, the car still buzzing. I felt like I wanted to crawl out of my skin, I couldn't catch my breath, and I had a constant knot in my throat just waiting for any reason to start crying about how fucked up everything was and how quickly our once normal, boring, beautiful life had disappeared. It is amazing how quickly you can go from living your everyday life with everyday worries like an empty gas tank or figuring out what to make for dinner to absolute hell and facing death in a matter of moments. I have found that this is one of the most destabilizing things about grief. How everything can be OK and then not OK so abruptly. It makes us feel completely unsafe, anxious, and like we can't even be still even just for a moment. You may feel like there is no safe place for you to land in the world or within yourself at the moment and I know it feels un-fucking ending. Know that every uncomfortable emotion you are feeling right now, even the worst ones imaginable, are temporary. So keep with me.

"Mama, can I watch Netflix? I am hungry," Jackson's little voice in the back seat startled me into reality, and I pushed in the key fob to turn off the car's engine. "Yes, sweetheart. You can watch Netflix. What do you want to eat?" I asked in the most tender voice I could muster. My sweet Jackson. He had also lost so much after his daddy's accident and he was just too young to truly comprehend the gravity of it all. His childish innocence made my eyes well up in tears. "Mac and cheese?" he said excitedly. As I opened up the car door, I realized that I had no idea if I had any food in the house to feed him since I had been living at the hospital surviving on large iced coffees and assorted baked goods from the café in the lobby. I helped Jackson out of his car seat, gathered his lunch box and backpack in my hands, and we headed inside. I turned on the overhead lights in the kitchen causing both of us to squint from the brightness. I placed Jackson's things on the marble countertop and noticed a fat pile of mail in the center of the island with several packages. I had forgotten about the mail since Ryan's accident and someone (I honestly have no idea who because I was in such a daze at the time) had been collecting my mail and making sure everything at the house was in order. The pile of mail was a symbol that the world kept spinning when my own world had halted to a harsh stop.

Officers from Ryan's police department had been coming to the hospital during the day to visit Ryan and bringing me cards from acquaintances and complete strangers from the community who had heard about our story. The writing in the cards was heartfelt, sincere, and personalized, each stating they were praying for a miracle with us and telling me to reach out if I needed anything. I honestly had no fucking idea what I needed except maybe a pill to help me sleep or a large vodka drink, both things I couldn't have because I was pregnant at the most inconvenient of times. The irony of it all. When your world falls apart, there isn't anything, anyone, or any words that will make the pain go away, but I found there were things that made the experience just a little bit better. I found when my friends or family just anticipated my needs and showed up with things like coffee, a baked good, or a gift card for gas that these things helped me without me having to use brain power that I didn't have. There were people who watched my boys for me when I went to the hospital, folded clean laundry that was just sitting in my laundry room and saw the need, went to the grocery store and filled my fridge without saying a word, and cut my grass unprompted. These actions made me feel seen and taken care of while actually making my life easier in a tangible way when I was tackling the big stuff, like whether I wanted Ryan to have certain dangerous medical procedures performed or if I wanted to put him on hospice. No one wants to think about anything else when they are dealing with these kinds of issues. As far as things people said that were helpful within this experience, I appreciated when people were just honest and transparent about how horrible the situation was without trying to make me feel better or fix it. I didn't want to feel better, I wanted to be witnessed in hell. The truth is, there is no silver lining when your person suffers a serious medical event or dies. I wanted everyone to just validate my feelings and emotions without offering solutions, unless I specifically asked. I wanted them to just let my fucked-up situation suck without putting a positive spin on the harsh reality and truth that punched me in the face each day. It was helpful when people asked me if I wanted to talk about anything else like their kids or the latest gossip. Being given the opportunity of an escape, just for a little while, made this impossible situation survivable. The moments that stick with me the most and were the most powerful, profound, and impactful were the times that people directly met me in my pain, even when it was uncomfortable and when words escaped them. I have learned that this is the most loving, unselfish thing someone can do; sit with someone in their worst moments and just settle in the despair with them. I'll never forget the people that met me in the darkness and allowed themselves to be enveloped by it with me. Perhaps those are the people and moments that you appreciated the most as well during your most difficult days. The moments that you didn't have to pretend or put on a forced smile. That your world could just tumble around you and you could just

BE without any judgment and without anyone trying to mend a reality that could only be witnessed and supported.

I walked to the fridge bleary-eyed to figure out what I could put together for Jackson to eat. I swung open the doors to reveal shelves packed to the gills with dishes and Tupperware. Yellow Post-its on the fronts, stating each of the container's contents. "Meat Lasagna," one read. "Vegetarian Lasagna," another read. "Brownies," another read. "Chicken Parm," another. "Salad," and yet another. I put my hand on the inside of the fridge to steady myself as the words in black Sharpie on the Post-its started to get fuzzy as tears flowed out of my eyes uncontrollably. The coolness from the open refrigerator hit the tears that rolled down my cheeks. The outpouring of love and support after Ryan's accident from his police department, the K9 community, family, friends, neighbors, and the community at large was overwhelming. I was so grateful, yet I felt sick to my stomach. All of this meant that something tragic had happened to garner all of this support. This time the tragedy wasn't a story I had seen in the news or had stumbled upon in my social media feed while scrolling. The horrific and unimaginable event was MY life and I would have given anything at that moment to not be staring into an abyss of grief lasagnas. You may also know what it is like to be completely overwhelmed by grief lasagnas; perhaps there are even some in your fridge or freezer right now. It is completely normal and you are completely justified for having mixed feelings about all the amazing, wonderful things that people do for you after your world falls apart. You're not a monster. You're not ungrateful. You're not a bad person for feeling any sort of way about all of it. It all fucking sucks and I get it.

The World Is *Still* Spinning and My Husband Is *Still* Dead

It was before sunrise on May 30, 2022, Memorial Day, just shy of two months after Ryan's death. The sun hadn't even risen yet and baby Leo was screaming in his crib. At five months old, he was still waking up multiple times in the night. I had tried with all my might to breastfeed Leo for a year like I had with his brother, Jackson, and had managed to nurse him all through Ryan's twenty-two days on hospice and had even made it through a few more weeks to his funeral at the end of April. But sometime after Ryan's funeral, my body completely stopped producing milk. I didn't fight it or try to do all the tricks to keep my milk supply up. I surrendered to the fact that this was not a normal postpartum period, and with the physical and mental toll that nursing a baby had on top of being a new widow and not eating properly, I couldn't blame my body for calling it quits. I was tired. I felt really fucking alone. The consistent help I received at this time was from my mother-in-law, who came to my home two nights a week without fail to help me with dinner and bedtime with the boys, which was also the only time I had the opportunity to have an adult conversation during the week. This support allowed me the space to breathe and get my bearings in the chaos of being a solo parent and being the only one solely responsible for two little lives. The nights that my mother-in-law would come to the house felt like just a little bit of the weight of the world being lifted from my shoulders.

I stumbled downstairs into the kitchen half asleep so I could make an 8 oz. bottle of formula. "Jesus Christ,"

I whispered under my breath as Leo's wails continued to louden. I clumsily scooped four heaps of formula into a bottle and poured warm water over the powder. It created a clumpy mess. I twisted on the cap, making sure it was straight so when I mixed it, the liquid wouldn't fly everywhere, and I shook the bottle up and down vigorously until no more dry lumps of formula could be seen. I hurried up the stairs and through the hallway into Leo's room, where I found him rolling around with tears covering his cheeks. I lifted him out of the crib "It's OK. It's OK. Shhhh. Shhhh," I said as I put the nipple of the bottle into his mouth. It took him a couple of seconds to realize that the bottle was even there because his mouth was so wide from screaming. He finally started sucking and silence filled the room. I sat down in the rocking chair and looked at my phone: 5:45 a.m., the earliness blaring back at me. I prayed that once Leo was done with his bottle he would go back to sleep so I could curl back into bed and sleep off the grogginess.

Trying to stay awake, I swiped open my phone and hit the Facebook app. Although this was before I had even met Anthony and shared our relationship online, social media was a breeding ground for pain after Ryan died. I immediately regretted my decision to open Facebook, as I saw smiling familiar faces staring back at me. People were enjoying life. They were at the beach, at BBQs with friends, or at the pool. Time was marching forward; the world was *still* spinning and my husband was *still* dead. My world essentially felt like it was in suspension, frozen in time, like a perpetual state of Groundhog's Day of grief. I hated and resented those happy families who had their husbands and fathers when my boys and I couldn't. They could be carefree and happy. That was an impossibility for me at that moment.

The grief lasagnas and everything else had stopped. The "just checking in to see how you and the boys are doing and if you needed anything" texts had stopped. The sympathy cards with encouraging messages and bible verses delicately written in cursive that once flooded my mailbox were replaced by outstanding medical bills, useless flyers for window and lawn services, and other mail addressed to "The Estate of Ryan Allen." My world had stopped, but everyone else had returned to their own worlds. My mother-in-law, Karen, and my sister-in-law, Morgan, were the two constants that I could depend on when everyone quietly, but swiftly, went back to their own lives and responsibilities. Meanwhile, I had a behemoth boulder on my chest that I was battling with no relief in sight. I swiped out of Facebook and clicked the side of my phone to turn on the lock screen. I couldn't look at any more happy faces when I felt so far away from that feeling. I had forgotten what "happy" even felt like. Tears dropped from my eyes onto Leo's sleep sack and were swallowed up by olive green fabric. *This fucking sucks*, I thought to myself. I missed Ryan. I missed our life together. "I wish you were here," I whispered to the portrait of Ryan in his police uniform that I could faintly see through the darkness in front of me, next to Leo's changing table. It still didn't feel real. I realized I was still rocking back and forth and holding a bottle to Leo's mouth with the other hand. I looked down at Leo who had drank most of his bottle and was now passed out in my arms, his mouth slightly open and covered with formula. You may talk to your person who is dead too because you long for them and the life you shared, especially in those early, dark days. Throughout this experience, I have longed for the beauty and comfort in my life before loss and I have talked to Ryan. I have told him I love him, I have cursed at him for leaving me here alone with our babies, I have begged him to come back, and I have even texted his phone to wish him a happy birthday. Missing your person and longing for your life where your person was alive is a natural part of the grief process. Communicating with your person is a way to stay connected to your loved one that is no longer here.

Broken Promises

After a funeral or memorial, most people go back to their normal lives while you are left with one of the most difficult tasks—picking up the pieces of a life and future that has been completely shattered. After a life-altering loss, like the death of a spouse, it can feel like you're trying to put together puzzle pieces of your old life that no longer fit together perfectly like they once did. There are pieces missing. There are old pieces that just don't fit in this new world without your person. And there are new pieces but you don't know where they fit yet. And you're trying to put this enigma together at a time when people stop showing up. It is one of the more ironic things I have discovered about grief and life after loss: the dust settles and you're finally transitioning out of survival mode and running on adrenaline and you're the most depleted, exhausted, confused, and in need of guidance—that is when everyone disappears.

On the day of Ryan's memorial at the end of April 2022, there were many promises made. People told me that they would continue to check in, that the boys and I were invited to different parties and events over the fast-approaching summer, and others assured me that although Ryan was gone, they would always be in the boys' and my lives and we would always be thought of and included. With the abundance of love and support that we had received during the entire ordeal leading up to Ryan's memorial, I was hopeful. It felt like we would have the continued support of those who had rallied around us so enthusiastically after Ryan's accident. But I guess there is such a thing as sympathy fatigue. I suppose that after Ryan died, people simply wanted to step away from the darkness that Ryan's family and I were still enveloped by. The truth is this: people in the periphery of a tragedy have the privilege of willingly stepping into the darkness for a short time and they also have the privilege to step into the light again. You may have encountered those who are close to you that you would have expected to sit in the darkness with you, will not willingly insert themselves into a situation where they are so close to pain because it is foreign and uncomfortable. Those who are in the most intimate circle of a horrific event do not have the option to step out of the darkness so easily and without a war. They are completely consumed by it until they find a way to fight and crawl their way out.

It isn't an easy task to willingly insert yourself into what I call the "trauma bubble." Ryan's accident and death had affected so many in a profound way. Ryan had made an indelible mark on many lives in his short thirty-five years of life. He had a big personality, an even bigger brighter smile, and he was admired and loved. I will not take away from the grief and loss that so many people felt from losing Ryan. And I don't blame anyone for wanting to distance themselves from the ripples of pain that echoed after he died.

The gravity of the hole left by Ryan's absence was so powerful that if you got too close, you would be swallowed up by it. The randomness of his accident and the horrific nature of everything that happened was a reminder to others that terrible things can happen to anyone, at any time. No one wants the constant reminder that a thirty-five-year-old vibrant man and father can be ripped from the world in an instant. No one, especially those in the prime of their lives, wants to be reminded of their own and their loved one's mortality. It is natural to want to step away from suffering. It is natural not to want to be reminded that life is fleeting and that we will all die one day. It is normal for people to return to their lives when they are not the ones most intimately affected by a tragedy. It is normal for the grief lasagnas to stop being left on a griever's doorstep and for the sympathy cards to stop overflowing their mailboxes. It is what we do as humans. We avoid pain and suffering at any cost. We move forward. It isn't anyone's fault. It isn't cruel. It is just life and the way of the world. However, if you are feeling hurt and alone right now because of how quickly all of the support has disappeared when you are still very much in the trenches of grief, I understand and I am so sorry. Although this is a normal thing that happens, it doesn't make it any less painful or jarring. Soon after my husband's death, I found myself with minimal people rallying around me and checking in. As much as the grief lasagnas had made me ill to stare at knowing they only packed my refrigerator because something terrible had happened, it was incredibly painful when everyone fell silent. My suffering wasn't optional like it was for others outside of the trauma bubble. Every facet of my life was altered by Ryan's death. Each inch of my life touched and twisted. Nothing unscathed.

After I met Anthony and our relationship became more serious, he spent every weekend with me and the boys. During those two fleeting days, it felt like I had a partner again. Again, a weight was lifted for a short while and would come crashing down on Sunday nights when I was thrust back into solo parenting. This meant multiple middle-of-the-night wakings to feed Leo, grocery shopping, laundry, bath, bedtimes, drop-offs and pick-ups from daycare, dressing, teeth brushing, diaper changes, paying all the bills, making sure the boys had everything they needed for school and daycare, and running a household on my own for the first time with two young children without Ryan. Although I had some hands-on help, I found the most difficult part of being a solo parent was the mental load of it all. When your spouse dies, you become the only person who has to carry the weight of all the familial responsibilities, whereas before this was a shared duty. This is a heavy load to bear. The number of things to remember and things to do in order to keep an entire household afloat while you're grieving and barely hanging on by a thread, especially when you're also a parent, is utterly exhausting. And I hadn't signed up to do any of it on my own.

Like many things in grief, it may just feel like we are screwed, but we aren't. It feels really shitty when the world goes back to their own lives after the mourners are done mourning and you are forced to start over at an alarming deficit because you're in the depths of grief. The grief lasagnas may have stopped flowing but it doesn't mean you are incapable of figuring this shit out. What I wish I had learned sooner on in my grief journey that would have saved me a lot of anguish and blaming myself for why people stopped showing up is this: when you're rebuilding your identity and life after the death of your person, there are no external forces that are going to save you or bring you peace and happiness. Healing in grief is an entirely inside job. Don't get me wrong: being rallied around and supported is beautiful, and for an acute period it can be an absolute lifeline, as it was with me. But at a point, it can provide a false sense of security because when the inevitable happens and people go back to their day-to-day lives, you will be left alone to face your grief and your life without your person. It isn't personal. I look back now and I am actually grateful for how things played out, although it was initially very painful. I was forced to learn how to live and manage life without my person on my own. And that lesson, although harsh, has been extremely powerful in finding my confidence again after Ryan's death.

Very soon after Ryan's death, I was pushed back into reality. Being in and out of hospitals and then hospice after Ryan's accident was not real life. I was constantly surrounded by people and was never alone. On the day that Ryan died, that night I found myself home by myself and the boys for the first time in months. I was the most exhausted I had ever been in my entire life. My bones ached, my eyelids couldn't even stay open, and Leo, who was barely four months old at the time, cried all night long. There was no one else to soothe him. I realized very quickly that I had no other choice but to learn how to do life on my own. I had to figure out a new routine and rhythm for our family that just included me and my sons. I had to keep food on the table, clean clothes on our bodies, and the lights on in our home. I had to make sure the cars were up to date on inspection and bring the trash cans out to the curb on Thursday nights for Friday trash day. It was all on me, and what once seemed impossible, started to come into focus. I did things messy and imperfectly. I delegated tasks where I could, like having my cleaning lady come once a week. I hired babysitters so I could take much-needed breaks from parenting. I ordered groceries online and didn't worry about cooking for a long time. I built my own support system when most people went back to their own lives and faded far into the distance. I found other widows to follow on social media and discovered resources, like this book, to consume so I didn't feel so alone in the experience and in the emotions I was feeling. Giving widows and grievers a safe place to land is the entire reason I wrote this book in the first place. I don't want anyone to feel as unwitnessed as I did in the early days after Ryan's accident and death. No one should have to feel that way. I hope you already feel more seen within your own grief experience by just reading the words on these pages. As I mentioned previously, I realized once again that my capacity and energy for life tasks were much lower than they once were because I was living with grief. Grief takes up so much space and energy, especially in the beginning. Some days you will find that just getting out of bed takes Herculean strength and fortitude, so it is necessary to give yourself grace and ease as you discover what your tolerance for life is now.

The Honest But Sad Truth

The honest but sad truth is that for most grievers, a lot of the support that you receive prior to your person's memorial or funeral will dissipate and then disappear after the ceremony and ritual is over. People go back to their lives as usual. Promises that were made will be broken. If you had a select group of people who kept showing up for you like I did, then you are very lucky. Many don't even have that. I want you to know that I understand that this is hard and that you feel lonely right now. But you also have everything inside of yourself to get through this hump. And that is truly what it is, a temporary moment in time. You won't always feel this alone and like everything in your world is wrong. We cannot change or control how people act and show up for us, or how they don't after our person dies. But what we can do is create our own support system within ourselves and in the new life that we are trying to create after loss. Here is a list of actionable steps to take that you can start implementing immediately to feel less alone and more confident while you pick up the pieces of your rearranged life after loss.

- Reach out for help. I realized very early on in my grief and trauma experience, in fact the first week Ryan was admitted to the neuro ICU, that the events I was walking through at the time were so much larger than me and that I wasn't equipped to figure out how to manage it all on my own. I found someone who specifically worked with individuals in grief and those who had suffered trauma to begin processing what I was going through. Reaching out to someone who specializes in grief, like a grief coach, therapist, or counselor, that truly understands the complexities of the grief process is crucial. It is never "too early" to start getting support.

- Become your own security blanket, because you're always more likely to show up for yourself. I have learned there is a difference between being alone and being lonely. Experiment with a variety of situations where you are physically alone but you are still enjoying that time with yourself. After Ryan died, I went on "dates" with myself and started seeing what the experience of doing things by myself felt like. When there were times I felt extra lonely at home, I created rituals that relaxed me and that I looked forward to. For example, nighttime was particularly difficult for me in the early days after Ryan's death. I started putting on a podcast or music during my nighttime skincare routine so I didn't feel the heaviness of a quiet, empty house at night. This time actually became a part of my day that I looked forward to because it was something I did just for me.

- Start prioritizing your physical, mental, emotional, and spiritual health and well-being. This may mean starting a new fitness routine, finding a therapist or coach that you can talk to on a regular basis that understands you and your grief, or connecting with other widows or grievers in your area.
- Delegate tasks that are beyond your capacity, prioritize the tasks that need to get done and let other things just be for a while if you can, and ask for help when needed, even if it means paying a babysitter for a couple of hours or asking a friend to watch your kids so you can shower and take a nap.
- Lean into the activities that bring you some peace and comfort, even if those feelings are only glimpses right now.
- Intentionally reach out to family, friends, and people in the community who can support you in your pain

and don't try to fix your grief. If you are part of a religious organization, this may include talking to a religious leader like a priest, minister, or rabbi, or others part of your religious congregation. This can also be a local support group for those that have been through the same type of loss (i.e., spousal loss, child loss, sibling loss, parent loss).

We want the world to stop spinning after our world falls apart because when our person dies, our world has halted. We cannot stop the world from spinning after a life-altering loss, but we can become our own source of steadiness and comfort when the world goes on living when our person is dead. Healing, growing, and evolving through this experience is painful. You cannot avoid the pain as much as you may want to. Leaning into the pain, the heartache, and the trauma that you hold is how you will be able to process all the complex emotions that you are grappling with that are hindering you from taking steps forward into your new life. Breaking down to then rebuild a strong foundation for your second chapter will enable you to carry your pain with more grace and ease. Unraveling isn't optional and my own unraveling wasn't pretty. The rest of this book will show you how to lighten the grief load and what is possible for you.

5 | The Unraveling

It was fall, which meant that October 14, the first anniversary of Ryan's accident—and the day that I lost everything that made my husband who he was—was quickly approaching. The early morning sun was shining and the air looked crisp as I drove home from dropping Jackson and Leo off at daycare. I admired the changing leaves on the trees surrounding me, morphing each leaf on the trees from a vibrant green to yellows, reds, oranges, and browns. I have always loved fall. It is my favorite season. I love the cooler weather, apple picking, wearing cozy sweaters, drinking pumpkin beer, Halloween, and the beautiful transformation that the world takes in the autumn months. October 12 was Ryan and my wedding anniversary and was the time of year he always took time off from work after working overtime in the summer when everyone vacationed down the shore. Before Ryan's accident, he had been collecting and saving different pumpkin beers for me because at the time I was pregnant and wouldn't be able to enjoy them until the winter. Fall had been "our" time. Now fall was a landmine for grief. If you've lost someone you love, there are seasons and dates that are landmines for your grief. Twinkling Christmas lights in the winter, pumpkins on porches in the fall, the first budding of flowers in the spring, or people barbequing and American flags swaying proudly in the hot summer breeze may put you into a tailspin, reminding you that the anniversary of the worst day or days of your life are approaching. Often our body will remember a date or time of year that is approaching before our rational minds and we will start exhibiting more intense grief symptoms preparing our body to fight or flee even though the danger or crisis is in the past. The thing is, grief doesn't care that a death or trauma happened two months, two years, or two decades ago. The body remembers and holds trauma. It is perfectly normal to feel an array of different emotions prior to a significant time period including being more on edge, sadder or "griefy," or even angry prior to a significant time period.

I clicked on the playlist on my phone that I had created after Ryan died and hit "shuffle." The songs on the playlist were songs that truly captured my emotional state after Ryan died. They were raw and sad. The song that came on as I drove up the hill to take the two final turns to arrive back home was about unraveling. It was about feeling like you're coming apart at the seams, being pulled in different directions by circumstances and people, and faking a smile to the outside world while you're crumbling from the inside out.

The lyrics echoed through the speakers. I couldn't help but feel that every word of this song felt exactly like what I was experiencing and the emotions I was embodying. Ryan's death made me feel like my entire soul had come apart and exploded from itself. I felt exposed, vulnerable, and nothing like my old self. There was a new recklessness about me that I didn't recognize, knowing that my entire world had been burned to ash and I had survived, like a rising phoenix. When you've lost so much of your life, yourself, and your future, it doesn't feel like there is much else to lose. In the early aftermath of Ryan's accident and death, I dared the universe or God to give me more pain to handle, like I had already built a fortress of despair around myself and there was no room for more or that I could handle whatever horribleness was thrown at me. Although a new challenging of the universe and recklessness are not part of the very confined and limited five stages of grief, as I explained before about the five stages, grief is the most human experience I can think of, and although there are so many similarities with the emotions that people feel when someone they love dies, there is no specific standard for what grief looks like or how people act within this experi- ence. Grief is humanness, and therefore the spectrum of emotions, feelings, and varying intensities of those feelings are all fair game and within the realm of possibilities when your world shatters to pieces. Every person's reaction to a death and navigating the world without their person is uniquely theirs. Saying a big "fuck you" and asking for more pain at my most broken point from God or the universe was part of my humanness in grief.

As the music floated throughout the car and enveloped me, I thought about Ryan. How much I missed him. How unfair it was that something so random and tragic had hap- pened to him when he loved life so much. He wanted to be here. He loved being a dad and he was so excited to see our boys grow up. All of those things had been taken away from our family. I started to sob uncontrollably in sadness, in frustration, in utter rage. Crying didn't seem to touch the expression of my agony as memories flashed through my brain like an old movie. Ryan playing in the yard with Jackson and Louie. Our wedding day. Dancing in the kitchen as a family to Disney music on a random Sunday night. Laughing and holding hands in the car together. Flashing. Flashing. Flashing. Flashing. I let out a guttural scream making the back of my throat vibrate as I hit the steering wheel with the palms of my hands four times. My palms stung with pain and I clenched the wheel to absorb the shock running through them, shaking my arms as I screamed one more time before the car fell silent and still. My chest expanded and contracted rapidly, catching my breath as I pulled into the driveway. My palms still ringing with a dull pain and warm tears running down my cheeks. My own form of coming apart at the seams, my own unraveling.

Grief Is a Needy Bitch

Grief and the agony that flows from losing someone precious to you is a living, breathing organism. Grief and the visceral nature of it, the physicality of it, needs space. This kind of agony needs to be respected, nurtured, and nourished. It needs expression, it needs to expand, explode, and morph into different energies and emotions. Grief is so excruciating because it is love that you cannot transfer to your person because they are dead. The love for our person is reserved for them and therefore there is no relief from the pain that this love causes as it cannot be given away. In the depths of grief when there is nothing else but the heaviness of it all, there is no separation or distinction between the love you carry for the person you lost and the pain that comes from losing them. The love and the torment are tangled and twisted within you all at once. This kind of longing and frustration cannot be tamed unless it is intentionally tended to.

You must love and care for yourself within grief by letting the pain take the many forms that it must and then find ways to release it into the world. This may look like anger, rage, frustration, sadness, emptiness, despair, anxiousness, or guilt. Many times in our grief, we stifle and push all of the emotions and energy down that are intended to rise up inside us and be liberated from our bodies, so it doesn't consume us. In mourning, we put on a pretty smile and nod our heads politely in public, so we make our grief and pain consumable to the masses. But inside, we are screaming. At times, we even make our pain more consumable for ourselves because we are afraid of what will come out of us if we let ourselves truly go into the darkness. We think that if we let ourselves dip into that ocean of sadness we will drown in it. That we won't come out of it. But going into the darkness is the only way back into the light. It is the only way to reduce the force of the torment that you may feel. You need to let the many faces of your pain have space to breathe and allow them to introduce themselves so they don't bury inside and haunt your soul. Allowing pain to breathe looks and feels different for everyone. It may look like letting out a scream in your car, garage, or into the dark abyss of the night. It can look like running until your legs ache and your lungs are gasping for air because physical exhaustion is the only time that your body and mind let the emotional pain come out and tears fall. It may look like waking up at sunrise with a cup of coffee and furiously writing in a journal about how unfair it is that your person is dead and how you want your old life back. It may even look like planning a fun night out with people you love and trust, taking tequila shots, dancing until you're forced to take your high heels off, and singing until your voice is hoarse to feel more alive when you've been consumed by death for so long. There are no rules with any of this. Whatever activity allows the emotions that you need to feel and let come to the surface be released into the world is what you make time for. Releasing the pain of your loss is now just part of life as a griever. As the pain comes in waves throughout your life now, after experimenting with what works for you in order to let yourself feel it, you'll know exactly what to lean into when the pain hits you again. Pain will ebb and flow as you go throughout your days, and figuring out how to let yourself embody the pain, shift and transform the energy of pain in your body, and then move forward will stop it in its tracks and prevent it from consuming you. In essence, you're building a repertoire of tools and strategies that help you manage the spectrum of experiences within grief in a more manageable and graceful way.

After Ryan died, I was desperate to get back a sense of control in a world that no longer felt secure, predictable, or safe. My entire life felt out of control. During this time, I felt a constant heaviness in my chest and body, like someone had poured cement into me. All of my emotions were always right at the surface, waiting for an activation or trigger, or for no reason at all to seep through. I cried. I cursed. I screamed. My mind raced a million miles a minute. I felt uneasy. I was constantly swallowing down a big lump in my throat so I didn't completely lose my shit in front of strangers. I was terrified about my future and what my life and my sons' lives would look like without Ryan. I was scared it would always feel this way, so heavy and dark. I wanted to find some relief.

I leaned heavily into physical movement in the aftermath of Ryan's death because it was the activity I had done in my life before loss that gave me a sense of calm and helped me feel grounded and confident. Lifting weights, running, and cycling enabled me to push my body to its limits, channel all of my pent-up emotions and energy, and release everything that made me feel weighed down. I discovered that putting myself through the physical pain of a strenuous workout dimmed my emotional, mental, and spiritual pain even if it was just for the hour that I was doing it, although I found that the positive effects continued throughout the day. On the days I pushed my body, I felt more in control of my emotions. The brain fog that trauma and grief had left me with would lift slightly and I found I could focus better, and the use of other coping mechanisms (like drinking alcohol) to ease being overstimulated became more infrequent. I was far from OK, but I was better on the days I worked out. In a world where there wasn't much that could comfort me, physical movement, weekly therapy sessions, and writing about my experience as a young widow made me feel just a little bit better in the intense, early days of heavy grief. I didn't feel the need to hide my darkness from the pavement, my garage, or the blank pages of a computer screen or journal. These things weren't phased if I let out what was causing my suffering in all of its fury.

In the acute stages of your grief when it feels all-consuming, managing your suffering is the best you can do. Have patience and grace with yourself in this season when you may feel eager to just feel better and move forward. This isn't the time to thrive. This is the time to feel shitty. This is the time to break so you can build in the next season. Survival and avoidance of a complete breakdown are the main focus. I kid, but if you're going through the loss of your person you know exactly what I mean. Every day feels like a war against yourself to get out of bed and just keep it together the rest of the day. Life is going to feel pretty damn terrible for a while, but you probably knew that. And how long you are going to stay feeling damn terrible is different for everyone. But there are things that you can do while you're waiting for the suffocation of the early mourning period to dissipate in order to ease the burden. The pain that comes from the death of your person isn't optional, but being absolutely tormented by it all is.

I Am Going to Ask You

I am going to ask you to do something that probably feels impossible right now. I am going to ask you to practice living again. I am going to ask you to do some experimentation with yourself knowing that doing these things are not going to feel good at first, or even for a while. They are going to feel like torture in the beginning because grief is all there is right now. But I promise that you won't always feel the way you are feeling right now and this is how we start being intentional with our grief and our lives. Ask yourself the following questions:

- What are some activities that brought you joy or lit your heart on fire before your loss?
- What are some activities that made you feel calm and centered before your loss?
- What are the activities that give you a little reprieve from the intensity of the emotions you are feeling in your life now?
- What are the activities that make it easier to live through your day no matter what is thrown at you?
- What are some activities, hobbies, or even trips that you've never done before or taken that you've recently been curious about, want to try, or want to explore?

- What are some rituals and routines that brought you a sense of control, security, and peace in your life before loss?
- What are some rituals and routines that bring you a sense of control, security, and peace in your life now?
- Or what are some rituals and routines you want to start implementing in your life now to bring a sense of control and peace to your life that you're currently lacking?
- What are the activities that allow you to unleash the floodgate of emotions that are stored inside you and help you feel free to cry, scream, curse, and truly show all the ugly and messy colors of your pain?

Once you answer these questions, I want you to start doing them as soon as possible and I don't want you to hold back. Run until your legs give out and the tears that you have been resisting can't be held anymore because you're too physically exhausted. Go to a rage room and smash plates, screens, bottles, and mirrors, and scream how unfair it is that your person is dead. Get up at sunrise and write furiously in a journal about what grief feels like in your body and how mad you are that your life isn't at all what you wanted or expected. Find support and vent and cry to them. You're allowed to be pissed. You're allowed to feel completely defeated. You're entitled to be the saddest that you've ever felt and you're entitled to feel like you won't survive it. Your person is dead. My person is dead. And that fucking sucks and there is nothing we can do about that. But you get to decide how you want this next part to play out. You can let grief consume you or you can decide to intentionally unravel however you see fit. And then you can begin taking control of your life again and regaining the peace and joy that death stole from you when your person died. Your grief demands to be unapologetically seen, felt, and expressed. So have at it, but know that you're meant to survive this.

6 | The Art of Practicing Living Before You Feel Alive

"Cheers!" I lifted my champagne flute to Anthony's old fashioned and we clinked our glasses together. "Cheers," he said calmly and smiling. We were sitting at the bar at one of my favorite restaurants in Peddler's Village called Earl's New American Restaurant waiting for our food. It was a few weeks away from Christmas and we had just finished our holiday shopping together in the village, our first real task together as a couple. White Christmas lights twinkled on the wooden bar among fancy alcohol bottles. The people around us were eating, drinking, chatting, and laughing. The spirit of the holiday season was palpable in the restaurant that December evening. I had forgotten how magical that time could feel. The way that lights cover the landscape and sparkle when you're driving or out for a walk. How most people that you interact with during the season are extra jolly. You can feel the excitement and festiveness in the air. I took another sip of my champagne and leaned into Anthony. "Can I have a kiss please?" I asked playfully. He chuckled and leaned in for a quick kiss. "That's all I get?" I said jokingly as I tilted my head at him skeptically. He laughed and kissed me again, this time with a bit more force. "Well, that was more like it!" I giggled as I grabbed my drink again and acted like I was flustered from our kiss.

I enjoyed exploring the shops and buying gifts for our family and friends. Anthony and I sipped coffee and laughed as we made jokes about how shopping around the holidays was like being on the show *Survivor*, because you had to bob and weave your way through the aisles to avoid crashing into people in the crowded stores. I had loved every moment of it and didn't want it to end. As the sun quickly set and the chill of early winter made me pull my coat up over my chin and mouth as we walked, we decided to risk being late to relieve the babysitter and sneak in a well-earned meal together, just us. It was the first holiday season since Ryan's accident and death. The prior year, I had spent every day with Ryan as he struggled to make improvements and ended up in the emergency room three times before being transferred to an acute care hospital for brain rehabilitation. That time had been agonizing and there was no celebrating or happiness. I saw the Christmas tree decorations and heard the holiday music on the radio and all I wanted to do was scream. I wanted all the extra glee of the holidays to be fucking over. There was so much fear, anxiousness, and an intense gloom that covered me everywhere I went. There was no room for anything else but death and darkness, but this season was different. It could be different now and I was intentionally choosing to explore the joy that was possible, instead of succumbing to the sadness I could easily bury myself in. You may also find yourself in limbo somewhere between feeling the most devastated and broken you have ever felt and truly embracing life again after the loss of your person. There is a season to be broken when your grief won't allow any room for anything but despair. But there does become a point in time in grief and your evolution within the experience of grief where there is more space to let some joy in. Here is your invitation to open the door for some glimpses of happiness when it knocks on your door.

Somewhere between the heat of the summer and the crispness of the fall, I had started to feel a shift in me. Like the changing seasons, my grief was evolving and morphing into something else entirely. I was busy preparing for the launch of my memoir at the beginning of the year and in the middle of a course to become certified as a grief educator in order to help others through their own grief in a few months. As a couple, Anthony and I were getting more serious, and he spent every weekend with me and the boys. We found ourselves talking more and more about a future together. Jackson and Leo were happy and thriving and I was getting a routine down during the week when I was on my own. There were still some days I felt overwhelmed and tired under the mental load of solo parenting while trying to navigate the new life and identity I was growing into. The parts of me that were healing from being in fight or flight mode for so long were easily annoyed and over-stimulated. But I was tending to those parts of myself through therapy, writing, and leaning into the activities that I discovered served as an anchor for my peace, stability, and comfort within the messy and rough terrain of grief. I found myself starting to feel like I was truly living again. I was beginning to feel confidence within myself like I was building a rapport with the woman I had become after Ryan's accident and death. I was proud of the woman I was becoming who was fearless, unapologetic, and passionate about what she was creating in the world.

This shift didn't happen all at once, but little by little. So slow in fact that I didn't notice the subtle changes that I was experiencing within myself and my grief on a day-to-day basis. I knew what helped my pain and I did those things as much as I could. I continued to go through the motions and rhythms of life even when all I wanted to do was lay in bed all day. I practiced living again before I even felt alive. Actively engaging in life even in the smallest and most trivial way after a life-altering loss is a show of faith and hope that there is still a life left to live, that life is worth living, and that there is beauty to be found here. This can look like saying "yes" to a friend's lunch invitation when you could stay in bed all day watching Netflix or returning to the yoga class you loved and went to religiously before your world fell apart. It can even look like allowing yourself to laugh when someone says something funny. You're allowed to have moments that bring you out of the darkness. In fact, you deserve them and you deserve to intentionally create more of them. This is how we continue onward with the pain of our loss, which will always be present in some form. We experiment with living again, even when it feels uncomfortable and impossible. We do what is hard and we continue doing it, day in and day out until the heaviness starts to lift and we can breathe, smile, and laugh again.

My grief was transforming while my new life was unfolding, but there still wasn't a day that went by that I didn't think about Ryan or miss him. I would think about how adorable and funny he would have been with our two beautiful boys and how much he would have adored baby Leo. How he would be advancing in his career as a K9 officer with his partner, Louie, and how he would be soaking in and loving every moment of it. I would think about the activities we would be doing as a family and about how much he is missing. I allowed myself to go into the crevices of my heart and mind where Ryan and my broken future was laid to rest. It was necessary to mourn what will never be. I had to come to peace and acceptance that the life that I knew, loved, and wanted to live would never be again. Everything I had planned and thought my future would be like had evaporated. I knew I had to go into the darkness to reconcile with these harsh truths, but I also knew I could bring myself out of it. In essence, I allowed living and grieving to co-exist and mingle in harmony with one another in a way that made sense to my new experience as a person living permanently with the pain of losing someone precious. I found myself dreaming again about my future and what my life could look like as well. I wasn't just going through the motions each day on autopilot in order to simply survive without falling apart at the seams. My pain was no longer right at the surface and I didn't wake up every morning with dread when I realized that my husband was dead. I mastered how to dip into the pain to process and integrate it into my new life and I learned how to take a break or respite from my sadness by fully embracing experiences and being in the moment, allowing myself to feel bliss, love, excitement, and gratitude. I discovered somewhere along the way that there is no completely "healed" from grief, but there was so much more to the story I was writing for myself than just sorrow. There is so much more to your story too and by practicing oscillating between being in the pain and taking breaks from the pain, you will find a balance that is authentic to you, honors your loss, and helps you process your emotions while also allowing for you to feel alive again.

★★★

Anthony and I were taking advantage of our rare break from the typical chaos of sharing our time together with a baby and a five-year-old. We had been dating for six months at this time and our weekends together usually consisted of tag teaming diaper changes, preparing a million meals and snacks for cute but demanding little people, listening to *Bluey* in the background, and managing a naptime schedule. Our courtship had been anything but typical from the beginning, and we were tackling dating and getting to know each other while parenting together. It was far from an ideal situation, but Anthony made me feel grounded, secure, and safe, which were all things I had lost and yearned for after Ryan's accident. Although my grief made me question so much of how I was feeling and acting because it muddles everything, I trusted how serene and at peace I felt spending time with Anthony. "Can I take a picture of us?" I said as I started to lift my phone in selfie mode above my head. "Of course," Anthony smiled as he moved his bar stool closer to mine and put his arm around the middle of my back. I leaned my head on his shoulder. "Smile!" I instructed and laughed as I snapped a picture of us. I examined the photo carefully for a moment. I had posed for so many photos after Ryan's accident and had faked so many smiles while it felt like I was slowly dying inside. When I look at those photos, I have a smile plastered on my face, but all I see is pain. The picture with Anthony sitting at the bar at Earl's that December evening after holiday shopping was different. I was smiling with my entire face again. I looked genuinely happy and content. I was beginning to feel some semblance of wholeness although a part of me would always be missing. It was unmistakable and remarkable after so much heartbreak. I discovered that joy and excitement can co-exist amidst sorrow. Creating and building a new life after the death of your person is about maintaining your autonomy and leaning into your true self as someone who has been molded by death and tragedy. Your true self looks different now because you are fundamentally different. Trust yourself that you know what shifts and adjustments make sense to you, your grief, and your life now. Most importantly, when you start feeling flashes of hope, joy, and contentment again, hold onto them. Lean into the activities and people that bring that magic out of you. Part of finding magic in your life after the death of your person is discovering who you are in the aftermath, learning to love the new person you've become through tragedy and deep heartache, and experimenting with what makes you feel like the most authentic version of yourself. The next question for yourself is, who am I now?

Things to Try

- **Do nice things for yourself:** Go buy yourself some flowers or treat yourself to a fancy dessert and coffee just because.
- **Go on dates with yourself or schedule dates or experiences with friends and family.**
- **Romanticize normal activities:** For example, just don't cook dinner. You can go to a market and take your time picking out the ingredients for the recipe you carefully picked out, get a nice bottle of wine, leave yourself plenty of time to cook for yourself, and put some music on when you're doing it. This is just one example, but *you can make seemingly trivial and mundane experiences really beautiful and special.* If you're a mom with young kids like I was when my world fell apart, making mac and cheese or chicken

fingers for them for dinner and putting them to bed a little earlier so you can take a nice shower and watch your favorite TV shows is also a version of creating pockets of peace, enjoyment, and self-care in your day-to-day life.

- **Create rituals and routines that feel supportive and allow you to feel both productive and in control.**
- **Experiment with different or new activities:** This can include going to a new workout class or starting a new hobby.
- **Put on music, a podcast, or the TV in the background:** Fill your home with noise and LIFE again.
- **Explore different places by yourself like coffee shops or bookstores.**

Remember, do whatever feels authentic to you. Only you can determine when is the right time to do some of these activities.

7 | The Scarlet "W"

Soon after the one-year anniversary of Ryan's accident, when I was simply out and about getting myself a coffee, I found myself on a whim, in a jewelry store located on the main strip in Doylestown looking for a new necklace for my life as a widow. Although I hadn't planned on purchasing a new necklace on that particular day, it felt like a necessary and symbolic step in moving forward and building a new identity for myself in a world without Ryan. What I had decided to wear around my neck since Ryan's accident had been significant for me. The first night that Ryan was admitted to the ICU at Penn Presbyterian in Philadelphia, his cousin Michael had asked me what items he could bring me from home. You may be thinking that the first thing I asked him for was a toothbrush, hair brush, or a fresh change of clothes. Those items would have been practical after all. But the first thing that came to mind to ask for while Ryan was fighting for his life in a hospital bed was Ryan's wedding band. In the hell I had been forcibly dropped into, Ryan's wedding band was the item I felt I needed because it was emblematic of our love and our history together, which made me feel closer to him when it felt like he was slipping away from me. I slid it on the necklace chain I had already been wearing as I desperately reached to feel closer to Ryan when he couldn't sleep next to me in bed or give me advice as to the life and death decisions I had to make for him. It felt like I was channeling him as I would clasp my fingers tightly around it, always asking myself *What would Ryan do?* and *What would Ryan want?* Strangely, this ritual gave me clarity and focus when things felt fuzzy and like the world was closing in around me. I prayed while holding Ryan's wedding band more times than I can even remember. I prayed to God to take me instead. I prayed to God to miraculously heal Ryan. And then when nothing else could be done, I prayed for him to die quickly and painlessly. Lastly, I prayed for him to be free, happy, and whole again.

After Ryan's death, I was gifted a beautiful necklace of a replica of Ryan's police badge with his badge number engraved on the back with the words "I'll love you always." This necklace felt like a suitable replacement for wearing Ryan's wedding band around my neck, which started to feel heavier and cumbersome after he died. A sign it didn't make sense for me to wear it anymore. A sign that I no longer needed it. I wore the new necklace of Ryan's badge for his memorial and wake, and through our first summer without him. It made me feel connected to him at first. It gave me some semblance of peace without him. But when the summer ended and I was taking bigger strides toward discovering who I was in the aftermath of losing Ryan, I felt that the necklace was mentally hindering me from moving forward in my grief. There were several encounters when I was stopped by strangers who noticed the necklace and asked about it. Each time I responded, "It is for my husband who was a K9 officer," my voice trailing before starting the next part, "he died this past April." I didn't have the energy to lie or sugarcoat my reality to anyone. I didn't have it in me anymore to make others feel comfortable at the expense of my own truth.

After your person dies, you are not responsible for someone else's comfort if this means sacrificing your own.

My bluntness always elicited a cross between shock and pity on the stranger's face, who had only asked so innocently about a necklace. The stranger would then quickly say something like "Oh! I am so sorry," and then turn away, avoiding adding more awkwardness to the interaction. I was always grateful for their speedy exit. I didn't want anyone's pity and I found it difficult to have normal interactions with even the most well-intentioned individuals who genuinely cared and wanted to help so soon after Ryan's accident and death. That's the really hard thing about grief, all social graces go out the window for a dark season and it is common to come off as cold, ungrateful, or even plain obnoxious. I'm sure I offended some people in this dark season, but the right people understood, gave me so much grace, and didn't hold it against me. I've found that the people that are meant to remain in your life through crisis and after the dust settles from tragedy will keep coming back, even after acting like the worst version of yourself. The truth is, I didn't have the energy to receive the kindness of others and show gratitude at the time. I didn't have anything left to give or the capacity for small talk. It was all exhausting and overwhelming. It is something that is difficult to grasp or understand until you're in it, but if your spouse is dead or you have gone through another loss that rearranges your world, then you get it.

As I made strides to establish a new identity in my shattered world, I found it difficult and painful that how I was unintentionally portraying myself to the outside world was wrapped up in being Ryan's widow, rather than being Whitney. It felt like wearing Ryan's badge around my neck was my own scarlet letter. Instead of an "A" for an adulteress like Hester Prynne, I wore a "W" for widow. I would always be Ryan's wife and widow, but I didn't need the entire world to see that "W" first. I yearned for a fresh page to start writing the next chapter of my life. I didn't need to wear Ryan's badge to remind me of the love we shared. I didn't need to prove to the world the devotion I had for him. I would carry my eternal love for Ryan until my last breath. A new necklace for this next phase of my life felt the most authentic to the woman I was becoming.

My thumb and middle finger traced up on the chain of the badge necklace as I glanced at the jewelry in the display cases. Everything sparkled from the fluorescent lighting in the store. I wanted something that was simple, elegant, and sophisticated without being flashy. "What are you looking for today?" the man behind the display cases asked. Without even looking up or thinking I said, "My husband died recently and I am wearing a necklace of his police badge but I really need something that feels like ME for this next stage of my life," I blurted out all in one breath. Again, in my grief, I didn't have it in me not to be completely honest and transparent. There were no euphemisms or wrapping the reality of my dead husband up in a bow for anyone. There was me, the jeweler, and a very long silence before I finally looked up at him as he stared blankly in my direction. "I see … I'm very sorry to hear that. Let me see what we can find for you," he said professionally as he started to eye the display cases. I appreciated the professionalism for this task. He pulled out a small black display with three different necklaces on it. I was automatically drawn to two of them. They were both white gold but one had several small diamonds all around the chain and the other one had one larger diamond center piece with a plain chain.

"Here is a mirror. I'll give you a few minutes to try them on," the jeweler said as he handed me a small black handheld mirror and then turned to walk into a back room. I started to try each of the two necklaces on in silence. I gently pulled my hair off of my neck and back and lifted my chin, turning my head back and forth as I watched the diamonds glisten and sparkle in the reflection. I examined each delicate piece carefully on my body. After I was satisfied with comparing the two necklaces, I started to lower down the mirror and stopped suddenly as I locked eyes with myself. My eyes looked different now than they had before Ryan's accident. Having lived all the experiences I had gone through over the last year and some, my eyes looked more mature somehow. Much older than my thirty-five years. They looked sadder too. Ryan's accident and death had taken so much from me and the traumas had taken that small glimmer of innocence from my eyes. The darkness that my soul held now would forever be reflected through my big green eyes.

I placed the mirror down on the glass just as the jeweler appeared again from the back room. "Did you make any decisions?" he asked matter-of-factly. "Yes. I'll take this one," I said, pointing to the necklace with the little diamonds around the entire chain that I was still wearing. "Can I wear it out?" I asked. "That one definitely suits you. And no problem. Of course you can," he said sweetly while he started to scribble the cost of the necklace on a pad of lined paper. I took out my wallet and ripped my credit card out of it. "Here you go," I said eagerly while he was still writing. I didn't even look at the cost. I knew the necklace was expensive, but I didn't care. This was the first big purchase I had made on my own without having to consult Ryan.

This was an item and decision I had picked out and had made all by myself. The start of many decisions, big and small, I would have to make for myself and our boys. It is scary to make decisions by yourself after your person dies because it solidifies that any decision and the consequences of those decisions fall solely on you. There isn't anyone to act as a sounding board or safety net to catch you when you fall. It is you making all the calls in your life now and it can feel both terrifying and freeing all at the same time. You have to be the one to catch yourself now. Trust yourself, connect with the person you are becoming, and the life you are creating, and go for it. The jeweler rang me up as I tapped my fingernails on the glass nervously and bit on my bottom lip. I was suddenly desperate for some fresh air. The jeweler handed me my receipt and credit card and I grabbed them from his hand and shoved them in my pocketbook. "Thank you so much! I really appreciate it," I hollered as I started to take quick steps toward the door. The bell on the door chimed so loudly that I didn't hear the jeweler's goodbye, only a muffled deep voice as the door shut abruptly behind me. I paused on the landing. I closed my eyes for a moment facing the street, clutching my new necklace as I took a long deep breath of the cool fall air. "Diamonds and pearls," Ryan's voice echoed in my mind as the air hit my flushed cheeks. It was something Ryan had always said jokingly. He would say that he worked so hard to keep me in diamonds and pearls. I wasn't all that fancy but the sentiment was true. Ryan had always done everything in his power to make me feel like a queen and throughout our ten years together, he had surprised me with many beautiful gifts. *You would love this necklace on me*, I thought as I smiled to myself with tears welling up in my eyes. "Thank you,"

I whispered into the wind, hoping that Ryan would hear me somehow as I took my first steps into what felt like my new life without him by my side. Ask yourself what tangible item you can display, use, wear, or carry that symbolizes your new identity and the life you are actively creating after the death of your person, making space for more comfort and calmness as you hold the pain of your loss while building your new life. As I was experimenting with what items and activities made my experience living with grief just a little bit easier and more manageable, I also learned that fate, the universe, or God can also put someone in your path unexpectedly that is an answer to so many prayers.

At the Heart of Who You Are Now

At the heart of finding out who you are and who you want to become in the aftermath of a life-altering death, you have to ask yourself some important questions and get in touch with yourself and your needs. This is something we suck at in grief because it feels like grief is all there is when you're in it. You need to make the space to start creating your new identity and your new life. I encourage you to write out the following questions and your answers in a journal or open up a blank document on your computer.

1. How have I changed since the death of my person?
2. What are the parts of me that are different now that I like about myself?
3. What are the parts of me that are different now that I don't like about myself?
4. How can I learn to like, love, or simply accept the parts of my new identity that I don't like?
5. How does my grief feel within my body now?

6. How do I want my grief to feel within my body?
7. What are the parts of my life that still make sense in my world after loss?
8. What are the parts of my life that don't make sense in my world after loss?
9. How do I want to honor my grief in this next season of life?
10. What are things in my life that I want to change?
11. What are my priorities in life now?
12. What are the things and activities in my life now that make me feel a little better within my grief?
13. Who are the people in my life right now that make me feel a little better within my grief?
14. What are the activities and people in my life that make my grief worse?
15. What in my physical environment needs to be changed to honor the season of grief I am in and who I want to become?
16. What are some experiences I can plan to look forward to in the future?
17. What are new activities I want to try?
18. Where do I need additional support in my life now?
19. What are some new places I want to visit?
20. What are some rituals and routines I want to start implementing in my daily routine that I believe will help me with my grief?

I know this activity was difficult because you don't want to imagine a life without the person you planned a future with, but I promise going into this pain has a purpose. In order to start building a beautiful life around your grief, you must begin doing activities that match your new reality. You need to start planning a future without your person because that is the harsh truth. I'm sure it has been a while since you have asked yourself what you wanted from life because grief robs us of so much magic. It robs us of taking steps forward, planning, looking forward to things, and our dreams for the future. So what is the next step you're going to take that feels right and authentic to the person you are now or you want to become? That first step for me was a necklace, but it can be something very different for you. It can be as simple as getting a haircut you have never tried before or as complicated as a cross-country move. It can be starting a new fitness routine that brings you some peace and clarity or it can be starting over in a new career. It can be getting the Botox that your husband would have never let you get if he were alive (yes, this is something I did personally). The point is there is nothing off-limits or wrong. You get to decide the changes, activities, and people that you want to incorporate into your life now. Keep or add the activities and people in your life that help with the heaviness of your grief and limit, make boundaries with, or eliminate the rest. Now is your chance to start dreaming again. Now is your chance to start experimenting with who you are now. Look over and examine the answers that you jotted down in the activity I asked you to accomplish. Highlight the first thing you want to focus on and work your way through the others at your own pace. The most important thing isn't that you do everything right or that you have all the answers, it is taking intentional action to find out what feels good to you in the world and life you are creating.

8

A Love That Feels Like Coming Home

I fluttered my eyes open, my head heavy on the pillow. My bedroom was covered in a velvety shadow and a soft light from the setting winter sky. It was peaceful and I was comfortable and warm. No part of me wanted to emerge from the cocoon that I had formed around myself with my plush white duvet. As I lay staring out the window, it dawned on me that I had taken a nap in the midst of my day and parenting responsibilities. "Shit," I whispered to myself. I had unintentionally fallen asleep after lying in bed for a few minutes with Anthony, after putting Leo down for a nap earlier in the afternoon. We had been "official" boyfriend and girlfriend for three or four months at this time. Yet, more than a year after Ryan's accident and months after his death, my body and mind were still recovering from being in constant survival and flight or fight mode. I was utterly exhausted. Usually, this exhaustion was accompanied by the feeling of being wired, my adrenaline still in overdrive because there was so much to take care of, so many responsibilities, and two little boys who needed me constantly. Most of the time I felt like a strung-out zombie with a million and one tabs open in my brain. I kept moving by copious amounts of coffee and a prayer. I hadn't yet gotten used to living by myself and sleeping in bed by myself, which just added to my anxiety, and thus my insomnia at night. I had gravitated to sleeping on the right side of our bed, which had always been Ryan's side. His absence was just that more palpable when the space that he should have occupied was empty. It felt right to take up the space that he should be. It was less painful that way. At night, when I wanted to sleep, my mind raced and that's when my grief liked to creep in the most. I often found it difficult to find a level of calm that facilitated actually falling into a restful sleep. And so I found myself perpetually tired and wanting to sleep when I couldn't sleep or wired, anxious, and grief-y at night when I could sleep. Perhaps you are also familiar with this vicious cycle after you have survived trauma. Every part of your body is exhausted and yet you cannot sit still or relax like you're getting ready to fight or run, or in my case to try to save my husband's life again. You may also feel like you're still in battle although the white flag of crisis and death is waving. You may still feel like you are fighting. I still felt like I was at war but this time my opponent was grief and PTSD rather than death itself. When I did fall asleep, Leo would inevitably wake me up at least two times a night and Jackson would always find his way into my bed, his little feet kicking me throughout the night. There was little rest for the weary. I never allowed myself to nap even though I was exhausted because my heightened state of awareness that I was responsible for *all the things* prevented this.

Needless to say, on this particular Sunday, I hadn't planned on napping, let alone sleeping for several hours while my four-year-old was still awake and my baby had to be woken up from his nap so his bedtime wouldn't get messed up. "Shit," I repeated to myself as I flung away my duvet from my warm legs. I tossed on the sweatshirt that was in a heap next to my bed, rubbed my eyes to readjust my contacts so I could see properly, and headed into the hallway so I could go downstairs and see what kind of state my house and children were in. I got to the hallway and started down the stairs, expecting to hear voices or at least the sound of one of Jackson's programs on Disney or Netflix. But I didn't hear much of anything. Just stillness and quiet. I finished my descent from the second floor, my heart thumping in my chest thinking there must be something wrong, and made the sharp left turn toward the kitchen. I noticed that the bright overhead lights were off in the kitchen as I entered, but there was a glow from the chandelier above the dining room table. I found Anthony sitting at the table with a large basket of laundry next to him and folding one of Leo's onesies. Jackson was in the chair next to Anthony with his container of Legos, building something. Leo was in his high chair cooing and twirling his little baby feet and hands with delight while watching Anthony fold laundry and his big brother play with Legos. The lights on the Christmas tree were twinkling in the adjacent living room and the TV was on with the volume turned so low I could barely hear anything. "Hi," I said groggily as I looked at the microwave clock to see what time it was. It was after 5:30. "Holy shit, I slept for over 3 hours?" I said genuinely in shock. "Thank you for getting Leo up, watching Jackson, and folding all the laundry," I said hesitantly feeling so guilty that I had dropped the ball on so much responsibility. "That's my job," Anthony said matter of fact, but sweetly as he bent over to grab the remaining items of clothing out of the laundry basket. The thing was, it wasn't *his* job at all. It was *my* job, but ever since I had met Anthony, six months prior, he had made me feel like I had someone to help shoulder some of the heavy load I had been carrying. Anthony started staying at my house over the weekends two months into our relationship when the logistics of securing a babysitter to be able to see each other got daunting and expensive. We surrendered to the fact that dating one another would also involve dating a cute but fussy baby and an energetic toddler. Anthony understood the reality of my situation and we committed to making the best of our time together. During the weekends he stayed at my house he made the boys and me pancake and egg breakfasts, helped change diapers, gave the boys baths, put Leo down for naps, raked the leaves in my yard and cleaned my gutters in the fall, played with Jackson, folded laundry, made Target runs with us to get home essentials, and any other chores he found needed to be done. He wanted to make my life easier during the two days he was with us because he knew how much I had to take care of on my own during the week.

I made myself a Nespresso to shake off the grogginess of my three-plus-hour slumber and sat in the chair next to Jackson feeling calm and even a bit refreshed. I had forgotten what that felt like. *Nothing had fallen apart without me*, I thought. In fact, everyone and everything had been cared for and loved. I smiled at Leo and then at Anthony who finished folding and piling the last pieces of fresh laundry. *Everything is OK*, I thought to myself. For so long my world had not been OK. It had been a hot mess really. I realized at that moment it was the first time since Ryan's accident that I felt like I could actually take a break or rest. It was the first time in over a year that my body and mind had felt safe and secure enough to fall asleep while the day was still unfolding, subconsciously knowing that there was someone else I trusted who was fully willing and capable of picking up my slack. This respite from the gravity of my grief, of the loss of Ryan, hadn't cured, healed, or fixed me from my pain. But it was another piece of evidence that the weight that I had felt viscerally and unrelentingly throughout my body could be lifted. At that moment I took a deep breath and it didn't feel like there was a boulder on my chest. A glimpse of relief. I was being held and supported in my pain and in my grief. It felt like coming home after a long and arduous journey.

A Love Tangled with Grief and Darkness

I began dating Anthony shortly after Ryan's death. I was still in the tender, tumultuous acute phase of deep grief and newly postpartum while processing and coming to terms with the trauma I had endured when I signed up for online dating. Part of me was still in shock and the other part of me felt like I had died with Ryan. Before Ryan's accident, I had been vibrant and full of joy. The little experiences in life felt magical to me. And in six months, I had morphed into a half-dead zombie. Nothing felt funny, joyous, or magical. My entire world felt enveloped by sickness, death, and a fucking grief that I couldn't shake as much as I willed it off of me. So much of myself had gone into loving and being in a marriage with Ryan prior to his accident. We had a beautiful relationship and life together. After his accident, all of my love and energy went into his care, and his potential recovery, and then when all avenues for his meaningful recovery were exhausted, my energy and love went into his peaceful transition to Heaven. Where does all the love for your person go when they aren't there to catch it and take it in? After Ryan died, with nowhere for all the love I reserved for him to go, love leaked out of me and revealed a gaping hole in the cavern of my chest that felt like an empty abyss and the weight of the world all at once. And so I sought out feeling alive again and not half dead, in the emotion and experience that had made me feel alive before Ryan's accident. I sought out feeling alive again in love, or at least the potential of it. I sought out giving the love that had once been Ryan's to possess in life to someone who could hold space for it. However, the kind of love I had to give after living through tragedy was engulfed and knotted with grief, trauma, darkness, and death that only a deeply rooted and patient man could weather and unravel. Opening up your heart again or even thinking about one day sharing your heart after loss is a tremendously brave act. It means you are also opening yourself up to yet another loss of someone you love and that feels un-survivable. But you cannot live your life based on waiting for the other shoe to drop. You must continue to live, take chances, and open up your heart again if that is what you desire because the cost of not doing so is more. The cost is never having a partner to walk through life with, which is one of the most sacred and beautiful things I have ever experienced, and if you've loved and lost you know what I mean. The important thing in opening up your heart again is that you find someone that can help hold and support your grief with you.

The First Kiss

"Hi," a deep voice behind me echoed before the sound fell flat into the cement in the parking lot. It startled me and I jumped as I attempted to get out of my car, grab my purse that was lying on my passenger seat, and my cell phone that was jammed into the cup holder. My keys dropped with a melodic rattle onto the ground. "Fuck. Shit," I whispered to myself as I twirled around in a frenzy to face where the voice was coming from. "Hi!" I said with a screak that was a couple of octaves higher than what I had intended. *Real smooth Whitney*, I thought to myself as I knelt down to rescue my keys. My now husband, Anthony, the thirty-four-year-old detective at the time, was standing in front of me trying not to laugh at how ridiculous I looked. I don't think there was anything in life at that moment that didn't feel like it had "shit show" written all over it. "Sorry, you scared me," I laughed. "I apologize. I saw you park so I just decided to walk over so we could walk to the restaurant together," Anthony said sincerely. I started to walk over to him. Anthony had tanned skin, dark hair, and dark eyes. His face looked young and kind. He wasn't as tall as Ryan, but he had a strong and serene presence. He was wearing a button-up shirt and jeans, his muscles pressed up against the fabric in the shoulders, arms, and chest areas. I was definitely physically attracted to Anthony, and our first date, which had been drinks at a restaurant called Havana in New Hope, Pennsylvania, had gone well, which led us to this particular evening and our second date.

Even before we ever met in person, Anthony and I texted and talked on the phone for several weeks. I had been transparent with Anthony about my situation, the horrors I had been through, and the fact that I was a package deal with two adorable little boys in tow. I figured I didn't need to waste a night out and pay a babysitter for someone who couldn't even handle talking about my reality. Anthony didn't seem phased by it all and he didn't make me feel like I was crazy for wanting to date. He took the time during our first in-person encounter to get to know who I was as a woman, and not just the tragedy I had recently been through. It had been so long since someone had talked to me like I was a whole person instead of staring at me with wide eyes and a cocked head like I was some sort of zoo animal. It sometimes felt like people treated me as if they could catch widowhood or tragedy like it was contagious or something. Anthony didn't look or talk to me like that at all. He made me feel at ease in my body, which was still vibrating with pain. He made me forget about my reality for a short while. "Shall we?" I gestured my arm across the parking lot like I knew where the hell I was going. We made our way across the parking lot, the wind pushing back my hair and giving me goosebumps on my arms. It was June, but on this particular day, it felt like fall. The Delaware River was next to us and it sparkled as the delicate evening rays of sun hit the water. "It's so pretty," I remarked to Anthony as we made our way to the restaurant for dinner. This was another instance since Ryan's death where I had noticed that I was more attuned to the simple beauties in the world. I was in awe of how sunsets splashed the sky with magnificent reds, pinks, purples, and oranges; the way leaves danced in the wind; the way my first cup of coffee tasted in the morning; how melodic the giggles of my sons sounded; and how refreshing a cool breeze felt on my face while out on a run. These were things in my old life that I would notice but that I wouldn't truly stop to take in and appreciate. They wouldn't fill me with awe and wonder like they did in my new life. The magic all around us became more magical and sacred to me after confronting just how fragile and fleeting our time here is and not knowing when it would be my last sunset. The beauty of what death taught me revealed in how I began to feel about life after Ryan was ripped away from me so unfairly. The fucked-up irony of it all.

Anthony smiled and nodded his head at my comment. Our evening was spent dining al fresco so we could enjoy looking at the water as we got to know one another. Anthony told me about his small, but significant family. His mom, dad, sister, and brother-in-law were an integral and important part of his life and weekly routines, including frequent Sunday family dinners. He described his duties and his day-to-day as a detective for the New Jersey Department of Corrections, his work as a volunteer fireman for the past fifteen years, and how he put an emphasis on taking care of himself physically and mentally. His values were aligned with my own, at least what my values had been in the past, all of which had stuck with me and had become even more important in the aftermath of Ryan's death. He was family-oriented, ambitious, and hard-working, and he was attentive and kind. I told him all about Jackson and Leo, my work as a medical malpractice defense attorney before Ryan's accident, and how I was self-publishing my first book about grief and life after loss. Our dinners of short ribs and mashed potatoes at the King George II Inn turned into spicy margaritas at a hole-in-the-wall Mexican restaurant up the street. We sipped on our drinks as we continued our conversation, this time having to almost scream to project our voices enough to hear each other through all the excited, drunken chatter and laughter that surrounded us. I had forgotten what it was like to just *live*. To go out to dinner and talk, laugh, and have a couple of drinks like there wasn't a care in the world. I had so many cares to shoulder, but on my second date with Anthony, it felt like I could lift them off of me for an evening. By my second margarita, I called it quits so I could drive home and relieve Morgan, who was in town for the night and had volunteered to man the fort of children so I could go out for a few hours. I noticed that my throat felt sore from shouting for the last couple of hours as we walked out of the restaurant. The door felt heavy as I flung it open toward me and a huge gust of cool wind blasted me on my face, the top of my chest, and my shoulders, which were exposed in the blouse I was wearing. "Whoo. It got cold," I said as I crossed my arms around my body to stay warm. We walked briskly to the parking lot. We continued to chat during our walk but I was distracted the entire time thinking about whether Anthony was going to try to kiss me and if he did what that would feel like. We finally got to my car and it was time to say goodnight. "I had a lot of fun!" I said to him. "Thank you for dinner and drinks. It was really nice to talk to someone who isn't a 4-year-old," I giggled nervously to myself not knowing what to expect next. "You're welcome. I had fun too," Anthony said calmly, literally the opposite of what I felt in the moment. There was a pause and Anthony moved closer to me and started to lean in. Instinctively I did the same and it felt like our faces moved in slow motion toward each other until our lips gently touched. My body went from being cold to feeling a rush of warmth move from my feet to the top of my head. My stomach did a little flip. *Butterflies*, I thought to myself. It had been so long since I felt that, since Ryan, and I wasn't ready to let go of that feeling just yet. We both pulled away slowly, smiled at each other, and kissed again, this time we were more comfortable and we pressed our lips together with more force. I slid my hands up Anthony's back, feeling his muscles, and squeezed like I was giving him a hug. He did the same to me.

After Ryan's accident, I learned that time is relative. Moments in time can feel like a lifetime or they can feel like a blink of an eye. It doesn't matter how much time is passing on the clock or the calendar, there are some life events where we feel like we are suspended in time and others when we are catapulted through it. When I kissed Anthony, like when I had kissed Ryan when he was alive, time stood still and everything around us melted away. I don't know how long we kissed, but we were only jolted back into reality by a car driving past us at a close distance, the sound of small stones crunching and crackling beneath the car's tires as it sped by. We separated our lips first and then our bodies. My arms around Anthony's torso the last to release and fall to my sides. Anthony smiled bashfully at me. "We should probably head out. Get home safe. We will talk soon," Anthony said as he turned to walk to his truck. "Sounds good," I said as I tucked a stray hair behind my ear, still trying to get my bearings. I hopped in my car and placed my hands on top of the steering wheel. I took a deep breath before grabbing my keys out of my purse and inserting them into the ignition. The soft hum of the car's engine purred as I turned my neck to start backing up from the parking spot. It was a thirty-minute drive back to my house and my mind quickly went from the elation that comes from having a good first kiss to feeling sick to my stomach. *Ryan is dead*, I thought to myself as I came to a halt before pulling out into the street from the parking lot. *Ryan is dead*, I repeated in my thoughts. It didn't take long before the warm, comforting rush from my kiss with Anthony was met with a pit in my stomach and a lump in my throat. I enjoyed spending time and getting to know Anthony. I really liked kissing him. And my husband was dead. I missed him terribly. I thought to myself how truly remarkable it was that elation, excitement, despair, grief, anger, joy, disbelief, shock, and so many emotions in between can be true at the same time. How my life was about living with so many different truths. Life and death. The good and the bad. Light and the darkness. Joy and sadness. Laughter and tears.

As I drove, my mind flashed to my last kiss with Ryan at the funeral home before he was cremated. How cool his lips felt against mine, how they tasted bitter with chemicals, how he couldn't kiss me back. No butterflies, just pure despair. I had kissed Ryan's lips, the lips I had kissed for a decade, but the kiss felt empty. Like kissing a hollow vessel. The difference between how heavy a soul feels within a body and how cavernous it feels without one is palpable. When I kissed Anthony, I felt the weight of his soul, his warmth, and how distinctly it felt like his spirit was contained within his body. The buzz and excitement from my kiss with Anthony flowed throughout my body at the same time it was flooded with my longing to feel Ryan's beating heart against the side of my face as I snuggled into his warm chest like I always had for one more embodied embrace.

Reach For the Good

I am in love with a man in Heaven and I am in love with a man on Earth. The truth is that if Ryan were still alive we would still be married. We would be happy. There is no question that we would be together until we were old and gray and one of us passed away if we had gotten the opportunity. I would have never met Anthony if Ryan was still alive. But Ryan is dead. Ryan and I cannot be together in this lifetime. And in the storm of my grief, I stumbled upon an old, mature soul that makes me feel anchored, grounded, and lighter within my heartbreak. I have found joy again. I have discovered peace again. And the pain that comes from losing the only other man I have truly loved, the father of my children, a life I was happy to live, and a future that I thought we would live out together, remains and persists.

Being in a new relationship has unearthed so many facets of my grief that would have remained hidden until and unless I entered into another relationship. The comparison, the guilt, the constant feelings of "wrongness" because my relationship with Anthony is not with Ryan, the man I had intended to spend forever with. Loving, kissing, holding, parenting, and planning a life with someone else is a constant reminder that Ryan is dead. It is really hard and it is really beautiful. It takes work and energy every day to tend to my grief and miss Ryan and also build a solid and healthy relationship with Anthony. Anthony is a remarkable person. He sees me as a whole person including the parts of me that have been molded and shaped by grief and tragedy and the parts that haven't. He took a chance on loving me when I was initially learning to love the new woman I had become after Ryan's death. He jumped aimlessly into dating a widow with two small children, knowing all of my truths and the potential complexities, and embraced it all with an open mind and heart. He has taken care of me and my babies since the beginning of our relationship and has forged on unwaveringly even when I pushed him away because of my grief and when things got really hard. Grief can make us destructive and careless in relationships because we already know what it is like to lose everything and survive. There have been several times in mine and Anthony's relationship when I would find myself in a wave of grief, missing Ryan, yearning for my old life back, and feeling so unsure about the steps I was taking into my new life, and Anthony didn't know how to be there for me because I didn't even know what I needed. He would be grasping to help me and I would get frustrated when he couldn't figure out how to make me feel better on his own even though I had given him no guidance. When I pulled away he would give me space and I would feel like he had abandoned me and get defensive. When he leaned in and offered love and advice, I would get angry that he thought I needed saving. In grief it can sometimes feel like there is no winning because you feel so much at one time. I would find myself questioning if Anthony was equipped to take on all the messiness that being with a young widow with two young children entails. I would ask him if he was sure that life with me and my boys was what he really wanted when his life was so simple and ours was anything but. I gave him an out on several occasions because I was afraid to truly open myself up to love again. I wanted him to be sure we were what he really wanted. We push the limits in relationships to make sure the people in our lives can handle the darkness within us because we know that another heartbreak may be too much for us to bear. But despite the times that I thought Anthony would run away because I was too much, or my grief was too much, or it was all just too messy and complicated for him, he assured me that he loved me and my boys and he wasn't going anywhere. He has loved me when I felt unlovable. He has loved me through the inevitable waves of my grief. Anthony deserves to be cherished and respected. Anthony deserves a woman who can fairly distribute her love between two men, even when the pain can feel all-consuming. Our relationship deserves the time, space, and reverence to evolve and grow. Anthony isn't responsible for my grief. My grief and how I carry it has always been my responsibility. It is therefore my responsibility to help Anthony know what I need within the experience because he deserves to make the right space for what I am going through. He is more than willing to make that space for me if I allow him to do so but I can't expect him to know exactly what I need in my grief at all times. That would simply be unfair.

Anthony cannot fill the void that Ryan has left in my soul. This chasm within my being cannot be filled. The weight of the love I have for Ryan and the pain from losing him can only be carried. It can only be taken up and tended to. No new love can fix or mend a hole that is permanent and only intended to belong to one person. This kind of despair, longing, and devotion for a man that I can never see in this lifetime can only become more manageable to bear. It can fade but it cannot disappear. I have moved forward because I have to, not because I wanted to. Finding someone to love and to be loved by after the loss of a spouse will not be the panacea to your pain and the darkness you hold. It really doesn't matter whether starting to date soon after Ryan's death was "healthy" or not for my grief and healing after my world fell apart. I met Anthony through online dating, so dating someone wasn't unexpected, but meeting someone so soon after Ryan's physical death that I could see myself building a life with was the unexpected part. Ryan was the perfect man for the woman I was prior to grief, trauma, and death charging into my life, and Anthony is the perfect man for the woman I became in the aftermath. Anthony has a calming and grounding presence that my brain and nervous system craved after everything I had been through. Ryan had been boisterous and larger than life, which I had adored before grief stepped in. But as you know, grief changes everything. Anthony's reserved, quiet, and serene nature felt like a compliment to my chaotic and complicated life as a young widow. Ryan and Anthony are the same or similar in important ways like in their integrity, work ethic, law enforcement background, and love for family. Choosing Anthony as my partner for this next part of my life was a conscious, deliberate, and intentional decision I made with my heart, soul, and the grieving and dark parts of myself that felt like he supported and made space for.

When your spouse dies, everyday feels like another day you can't come home. It feels like an endless bad trip or terrible nightmare and there is no comfort or safety net. I knew I had met the right person for me and my boys in our new life when it felt like I had come home again. Not home in the sense of a place or physical location, but coming home to a person and a feeling I had lost when my person died. Comfort, contentment, and a lightness I hadn't felt since my world fell apart. I had found my person again in the darkest place I had ever met myself in, in grief and my shattered life and future.

Nothing makes sense when your entire world implodes. There is no magical moment when we become ready to open our hearts up again to the possibility of love and thus heartbreak. There are no rules or "rights" or "wrongs" on how we choose to make sense and find some glimpses of peace in a life that no longer feels like it is ours. There is only trying to find and cling to the people, experiences, activities, and things that make us feel just a little bit less like we want to crawl out of our skin.

I share this part of my story, not because dating and being courageous enough to explore the possibility of love after the loss of a spouse is what you should do. Again, it will not be the "thing" that saves you from your grief. I'm sharing my own experience because falling in love and finding a new partner has been part of my life after my husband died. But there is no wrong way to write your second chapter after a life-altering loss. There is no singular road to finding joy, solace, and some lightness in the aftermath of death. You are going to make mistakes, in relationships and otherwise, as you figure out what feels right for you in the life you are creating after loss. I know because I've made plenty of them. It is going to be messy and ungraceful. It is going to hurt, a lot. But you're going to get yourself up, even with all the uncertainty, pain, and how scared you may feel and you're going to keep trying to reach for the light. Reaching for the light looks different for everyone. But it is your right to start feeling like you're living again. The beauty of being completely stripped of your identity, of who you thought you were, and what you wanted in life when the world crumbled beneath you is that every possible outcome is now available to you in your life. You can decide to date or not. You can do whatever feels authentic to you, knowing that at any time you can stop if something doesn't feel true to your grief and your tender heart. You are learning to live in an unknown world and that takes time. It takes giving yourself grace, patience, and ease to embrace that you won't have all the answers right away or ever. But you can be brave enough to try to figure out how to take just one step forward. The love I have found in the aftermath of my husband's death is simply illustrative of the good that can come into anyone's life unexpectedly after a loss-altering loss. So ask yourself, what is the good that you can reach for in your own life? Inevitably as you start reaching for the good in your life after your person dies, it will feel uncomfortable because the person you love isn't there to share the joy and new experiences with you. Feeling guilty for moving forward and finding some semblance of normalcy after loss is expected if not inevitable within the experience of grief. But guilt doesn't have to control you and prevent you from progressing and living.

Things to Consider If You're Thinking About Dating After Loss

I don't think anyone is ever completely "ready" to open themselves up to the potential of love after the loss of a spouse/partner. You're also never going to be 100 percent "healed" in your grief experience, and no matter how long you wait to date after your spouse has died, you're going to have to face aspects of your grief that dating and being in a relationship bring up. So instead of trying to figure out if you're "ready" to start dating again, ask yourself these questions:

- Do you have a desire to discover what the experience of dating is like?
- Where is the desire of dating coming from? Is it coming internally from wanting to explore the potential of falling in love again? Is it coming from external pressure? Is it coming from a desire of not wanting to be alone? Is it coming from wanting to feel alive again? It is coming from a place of wanting to feel desired and loved again? There isn't a wrong reason for wanting to date again, as long as it is a desire coming from you and you understand that dating is not a fix for grief.
- Do I have a healthy curiosity around the thought of dating and falling in love again? This experience is going to be scary and difficult no matter what, but it doesn't mean it is necessarily "wrong."

- What does it feel like in your body to think about dating again or when you're out on a date? Are you excited? Do you have butterflies? Or are you running to the bathroom during the date because you're overwhelmed, anxious, or holding back tears? Always trust what you feel (get in touch with your gut instincts again!), and I promise you will know if continuing is worth the work and the necessary growth and expansion you will need to experience loving someone after loss.

Just remember that dating and falling in love will not be the thing to fill the void (nothing can fill the void of losing your person), although the right person will bring so much positivity to your life. Do what works for you on your time table. There isn't a wrong way to do this, and you can always stop or pause if something doesn't feel in alignment.

9

It's Not About a Refrigerator

I started to feel the anger, sadness, and frustration bubble up inside of me. "We are taking my refrigerator when we move!" I said harshly with my back turned toward the sink as I fumbled to clean dirty dishes from the early morning breakfast rush with Jackson and Leo. The New Year had just recently passed and Anthony and I had been dating for close to eight months, and we were starting to look at new houses to buy together. Anthony's back and forth every weekend from his home in New Jersey was starting to become more and more difficult as our time as a couple rolled by. It got harder for him to leave me and the boys on Sunday nights after having a routine together over the weekends, and we missed him when he left. I felt that Jackson and Leo needed more consistency with our time altogether and that it was confusing and upsetting to them that Anthony would come and then leave for days at a time before returning. We were at the point in our relationship when we had completely committed to each other and we were talking about getting engaged, a wedding, a honeymoon, and even having a baby together one day. I was taking so many steps forward in my new life after Ryan's death and I was equally terrified, excited, and grieving over leaving so many parts of my old life behind me. There were so many emotions I was feeling all at once about these big life-changing transitions.

This particular morning, however, I was fighting about refrigerators with Anthony. "But it doesn't make sense to take your refrigerator when we move. We will leave this one for whomever buys your house and we will have the one that people leave in our new house. That's usually the way it works," Anthony said calmly and rationally. I looked at him dumbfounded getting even angrier that he just saw a refrigerator and didn't see or feel what I felt. He was right of course. It was all so rational. This would be my third move to a new home in ten years and I had never moved any large kitchen or household appliances. But I also couldn't bear to think about getting rid of my refrigerator because it wasn't just a refrigerator to me. The refrigerator that was in my old kitchen was the last big purchase that Ryan and I had made together before his accident in October 2021. The simple afternoon, on a weekend we had spent as a family at Best Buy making that purchase, stood out in my mind because it occurred so close to when my world fell apart. It was one of the last of a handful of outings we had done as a family. I remember Ryan talking to the salesperson about our refrigerator needs. I remember Jackson running around the store being cute and asking about and opening up all the different appliances we passed. That damn refrigerator was purchased on a Best Buy credit card and was the first bill that I had to figure out how to pay the minimum payment for after Ryan's accident. I performed this task as I balanced my computer and Ryan's old school checkbook on my lap with my growing pregnant belly in the hospital lobby while Ryan fought for his life on the fifth floor of the neuro ICU. So it wasn't just a refrigerator. It symbolized my life with Ryan. A world when my existence did not include having to contend with grief and trauma. You may also be keeping or holding onto items in your home that remind you of your life before your person died. It may be as big as a refrigerator or as small as a toothbrush. There is nothing wrong with keeping these items if they bring you peace and comfort. However, if they are hindering you from moving forward and stepping into your new life after loss, then it may be time to consider what items you can let go of. When an item begins to activate more pain and stagnation in your journey rather than peace and progression, this is a good indication you are ready to part with something. As discussed earlier, I knew when Ryan's things in our home made me feel like I was living in a tomb of a life that was no longer my reality. I knew from the pain I felt when living among those items when I needed to start going through his things. Just a reminder that along with so many things in grief, the ritual of going through, donating, or disposing of a loved one's physical items or items that were part of a home you shared is not easy or linear. You don't have to do everything at once. Life has a way of progressing and marching forward in a way that will naturally let you know when it is time. Again, trust yourself and your intuition in all matters. It is never "just" a thing. It is so much more than that and I know how difficult it is to release these items.

With so many things changing in my life now including a new relationship, new career, new book, and now an impending new home to share with someone, I was holding onto a physical object that grounded me to what my old life had looked and felt like in the "before." "I need a minute," I said to Anthony now much softer as I dried my hands with a dish rag and walked out of the kitchen, through the hallway, up the stairs, and into the hall bathroom. I placed my hands on the cool black granite of the sink countertop and looked up into my reflection staring back at me. I saw tears well up in my eyes and I held them back feeling silly that I had picked an argument with my boyfriend over a kitchen appliance that really didn't matter. I knew what the real problem was. Ryan was still dead and white-knuckling parting with any physical item, no matter what memories were attached to it, wouldn't bring him back. I realized that I was holding onto a ghost in the form of a refrigerator and it was OK to let go.

Letting Go of the Darkness

With the ball dropping in 2023, another wave of grief crashed into me harshly and unapologetically. It knocked me right on my ass and I experienced a resurgence of many of my early grief symptoms: a heaviness in my chest and belly, anxiety and fear, carrying a constant lump in my throat that was ready to erupt into tears at any moment, and a deep, deep sadness. The new year had caused me to viscerally feel the passage of time without Ryan into the next year from the year he had died. Having to say, "He died last year," felt strange and made me uncomfortable. Around the same time, I found myself feeling guilty for being excited about planning and taking steps forward to start a new life with someone else. With time passing like a relentless beast, causing my grief to be palpable while experiencing so many changes all at once, I couldn't help but feel like I was leaving Ryan and our life together behind. The guilt of being happy, finding love again, and living life without him covered me in a heavy and dark drape of guilt.

In the midst of building a life around my loss, I was losing my grasp on the sheer agony and despair that I had felt in the early days of my grief and I was able to embody joy and hope again. I no longer had to fixate on the past to find some peace from the wreckage of what had been my beautiful life and I was looking to the horizon to a new life, even if it was without my husband. But there was guilt intertwined with letting go of the sadness. These questions haunted me as I began to feel flashes of joy: "Will I lose my connection to Ryan if I release the heaviness of my grief? If I love my life now, will that mean I am not honoring the life that I shared with Ryan?" At the beginning of 2023 with the return of my heavy grief, I found myself desperately holding onto the depths of my sorrow because it was easy to connect to my love for Ryan there because my love for him was so bound up in my loss and heartbreak. When the guilt would creep in as I took steps into my second chapter, I thought about Ryan's and my heavenly reunion. I thought about the first words I would want him to say to me when that time came and I always envisioned him saying, "I'm proud of you." These thoughts or perhaps even premonitions gave me the confidence to continue building a life that Ryan was not a part of but that he would be proud of me for. This helped ease my guilt tremendously, knowing that I was doing exactly what he would have wanted. I also reminded myself that I had not chosen this new path for myself, that it had been thrust upon me unwillingly. I had not chosen for my husband to have a terrible accident and die, and I had not chosen to walk away from my old life that I loved living. I hadn't been given a choice in any of it, but I did have free will when it came to how I decided to move forward in the aftermath. I was truly able to let go of the guilt surrounding finding happiness and moving toward a new life without Ryan when I discovered that mourning wasn't the only way I could connect with him. I found that I could commune with Ryan through laughter, peace, and living a beautiful and authentic life for myself and our sons.

This connection felt more powerful and pure because it wasn't tainted by anguish. It was just pure love because it was how Ryan had lived his thirty-five years of life.

You may feel guilty and like you are betraying the person you loved by letting go of the darkness you carry from their death. Within your suffering is a connection to your person because your pain flows directly from and as a result of the death of your person. The dark shade of grief can become comfortable and familiar, even when it brings you misery because there is a connection with your person within that sphere. You may think that deep, visceral grief is the safest and most direct portal to the person you love. And yet there is a better way. Suffering isn't the only path to connection within grief. The purest way to connect to and honor your person is through doing something they cannot, which is to live fully and embrace that life is a gift that can be taken quickly and unfairly. In this way, you can release the guilt associated with moving forward into your life after loss and you can create an even deeper and more meaningful bond with your person. Discovering the connection with your loved one through the light rather than the darkness allows you to knock down the wall that guilt can create within grief. It allows you to see that you can release the sorrow without releasing the love. Death doesn't extinguish love. Death doesn't extinguish connection. Death is not the end of the relationship with the person you love, even though they are not physically here to live life with you. Some of the most comforting and profound experiences after Ryan's death have involved finding ways to maintain our love, connection, and relationship that transcend physical presence and even logic and reason.

Releasing What Is Holding You Back

I want you to reflect on your story of guilt and/or what you are holding onto that is preventing you from taking steps into your new life after loss. I want you to reflect on everything you feel guilty about, or fearful about, or where you are feeling resistance in the context of creating a life without your person. I also want you to reflect on ways you can connect with your person that is distinct from feeling the visceral pain of your loss. This may mean participating in an activity they loved, playing their favorite song, telling the stories or jokes they loved to tell, wearing their clothes, cooking their favorite meal, or toasting with their favorite cocktail. Here are some mantras that may be helpful to remind yourself as you're doing this activity:

- "I don't have control over life or death."
- "My person did not die because of anything I did or didn't do. I am not responsible."
- "My person knew how much I loved him/her."
- "I did the best I could under unimaginable circumstances."
- "I am human and therefore I am imperfect and life is messy."
- "I am making room for myself in my life now to release what is no longer serving me so I can move forward."
- I am deserving of a beautiful life.
- I don't have to hold onto the pain to connect with my person.

10 | Wings to Fly

At the end of the first summer after Ryan's death, I found myself at a crossroads. I was deciding whether to go back to the law firm I had worked for as a medical malpractice defense attorney prior to Ryan's accident or take a huge risk and start my own business as a writer and grief coach. I felt so different after Ryan's death and my priorities had shifted. My time here felt fleeting, fragile, meaningful, and urgent. I found myself feeling so much more deeply about life and how I wanted to live out my days. All my emotions felt more powerful and intense. My beating heart in my chest felt like an invitation to live a life full of passion and purpose. Ryan's death had completely shattered my heart, opened it up, and expanded it in a profound way. So much so that I just didn't know if I could go back to a career in law when it didn't light my heart on fire and I knew just how precious my time living was. I had absolutely no evidence that I would succeed in doing my own thing, but I felt a push to explore taking a leap of faith and creating an entirely new career for myself. Around the same time, a friend had given me the name of a tarot card reader that she highly recommended. I didn't really have a strong belief in the power of tarot cards and had never had a reading, but something nudged me to call her and schedule an appointment. I figured the worst that could happen is that I end up with no concrete answers or at best it could give me a bit more clarity on my career decision.

The tarot card reader, Judy, had agreed to come to my home to meet with me. The afternoon that she arrived, I saw her car pull up in the driveway from the big windows in the living room and my heart started beating faster in my chest. I had been fine thinking about the reading prior to

Judy's arrival, but I found I was nervous as I saw her open her car door and step her foot on the driveway. I didn't know what to expect. I went to the front door in order to greet her. I opened the door just as she was stepping up onto the front porch, the same step I had found Ryan unconscious on the day of his accident. I couldn't look at that step without a flash of Ryan's lifeless body slumped over on itself. "Hi!" I said excitedly trying to hide my nervousness. "Hello dear," she said calmly. Her curly, brunette hair flowed in the wind. She was dressed casually in jeans and a flowy printed top. "Please come in," I gestured my hand into the house. "I have to admit. I am a little nervous about our reading today," I figured clearing the air would ease my jitters. "Oh. There is nothing to be nervous about," she said reassuringly. "OK. Thank you. I appreciate that. Does the dining room table over there work?" I said as I pointed my index finger in the direction of the chestnut brown table just beyond the living room. "That looks great. I have to tell you that I usually don't travel for readings, but for some reason, I felt compelled to come here," Judy said as we walked toward the dining room table. "Oh wow. I didn't realize that. I truly appreciate you driving all the way from the city. I know the traffic can be brutal," I said smiling. "You're telling me," Judy laughed as she started to take out some items from her floppy large pocketbook. I sat down with my hands clasped together on the table waiting anxiously for instructions as Judy continued sorting through her bag. "So how does this work exactly? You just read my tarot cards?" I asked. Judy stopped looking in her pocketbook for a moment and stared in my direction before responding. "Oh well, yes, tarot cards are part of the reading if the guides tell me they could help, but I am a medium," she said matter of fact. My heart started to beat faster again. I hadn't known Judy was a medium and although I was open to the experience, I hadn't mentally prepared myself for a medium reading. My mind instantly thought of Ryan. *Maybe he planned this entire thing,* I thought to myself. Ryan had been resistant to believing in things he could not understand or that he couldn't rationalize. He was a questioner in all things and he always pushed the people in his life to have answers as to why they had certain beliefs or views. As his wife, it was annoying at times because where Ryan saw the world in black and white and right and wrong, I have always viewed the world more in the gray, with a belief and intuition that life is so much more complex than what is right in front of me. I hoped that in Ryan's death, he now understood that there is so much more to life and death than what he believed during his lifetime.

After Ryan's death, I sat with one other medium who had reached out to me personally. The reading she gave me was extremely validating and it had given me a lot of peace. After that reading, I decided that I wasn't going to seek out any more medium readings because I knew it would only cause me to continue to look for more answers and validation in the external. I wanted to force myself to find solace and answers within myself because I knew intuitively that was where true healing and growth could be found from my loss. My life now is evidence that this is true. Despite not intentionally seeking out any more readings, I found myself serendipitously sitting next to Judy the tarot card reader and medium. Judy finally sat down in the chair, adjusted herself with her legs and feet pointed toward me, closed her eyes, and took a deep breath. She then opened her eyes and looked at me for a few seconds in complete silence. I sat in a daze staring directly at her waiting for her to speak. "There is a young man behind you. He looks to be in his thirties. And he is wearing some sort of uniform. Maybe a military or police uniform? I can't tell exactly but he is definitely showing me some sort of uniform connected to him. Does this mean anything to you?" My heart dropped to the depths of my belly. Judy had no idea who I was, who Ryan was, or anything about what had happened. But it sounded like Ryan was standing right in the back of my chair. "It does make sense," I said as calmly as possible and I waited anxiously for her to continue. "He is also showing me children. Does this man have kids? I see two. Both boys," she continued. "Yes. He has two boys," I said trying not to show my complete disbelief. My heart was now beating so hard in my chest that I thought Judy could even hear it, but she wasn't fazed. "Okay. He is showing me an event that happened really fast that was connected to his death but that he lingered for a while. He didn't die right away," I held my breath and nodded my head, tears now welling up in my eyes. Judy giggled to herself and continued, "Sorry he is jumping all over the place. He is a really happy guy, isn't he? He is making me want to smile and laugh even though we are talking about something so serious. He doesn't want you to be upset. He knows how hard it has been for you and he hates that he can't be here to help and comfort you," Judy said as she closed her eyes again and took a deep breath to recenter herself. "My little engine that could" he is saying to me. He said you're my little engine that could," she said without emotion. I smiled, more tears welling up in my eyes as this was something Ryan had said to me on occasion and something I had never told anyone that he would say.

"OK. He is showing me a changing table with a baby and he is at the end of the changing table making funny faces and smiling and the baby is laughing at him. Does this make sense to you?" "Yes. That makes complete sense," I responded, my voice cracking now fiercely holding back tears. What Judy had said did make complete sense. Since Leo's birth, he had moments when he would look like he was staring off at nothing and he would start laughing. Notably, this had happened while I held Leo next to Ryan's death bed while he was on hospice in the couple of days leading up to his death. I looked down and softly whispered to Leo, "Say hello to daddy for me." I had always believed these were visitations from Ryan, his soul interacting with his son whom he never got to meet while he was healthy. This thought made my heart burst and break all at the same time. "Can you tell me who this man is?" Judy asked now looking straight at me. "Yes. It is my husband, Ryan. He was a K9 officer in Montgomery County and died in April of this year from a severe allergic reaction to a bee sting," it was hard to get all the words out. Judy looked at me for a moment with shock on her face. "Holy shit," she said still staring at me. "I had no idea. I am so sorry," Judy said genuinely in shock as she tried to regain her composure. I don't think she was expecting the person who had appeared at the beginning of our reading to be so closely connected to me.

Judy straightened herself in the chair and clasped her hands together, again taking a deep inhale and exhale before continuing. "He is showing me that you are on a precipice right now and he is showing me that you're afraid to jump. You are starting something new. He is showing me that you are writing and something with business. Entrepreneurship,"

Judy stopped talking and looked at me. I was frozen. Judy caught her breath and continued. "He wants you to know that you will succeed in what you are doing or what you want to do. He is showing me that whatever business venture that you want to undergo will be bigger than you even anticipated. You're destined for a lot of success in this area. You are going to make a big difference in so many people's lives," Judy said softly and confidently. She continued, "He has big white wings in his hands and he is placing them on your back. He wants you to take the leap because your wings will catch you. He will be with you each step of the way and help you in any way he can." I looked behind me and couldn't contain my tears any longer. I started bawling. Judy quickly grabbed her bag that was placed on the floor and started to quickly rummage through it. "I always bring tissues with me to readings," she said as she took out her wallet and sunglasses from her bag and placed them on the table in a quest for tissues. "It's OK. I'm OK," I cried as I sniffed hard to avoid warm snot running out of my nose and wiped the tears from my eyes, leaving little black puddles on my fingers from my mascara. *Wearing mascara that wasn't waterproof was a bad idea*, I thought to myself. Judy was finally able to find the small plastic envelope of tissues in her bag and she gently handed one to me. I blotted my cheeks and the corners of my eyes with the tissue and finally blew my nose. I composed myself and looked at Judy.

"Thank you so much for this reading. I wasn't expecting this today but it was exactly what I needed to hear. You have no idea," I said and then gave a big sigh. Judy's reading had given me so much clarity and peace. I felt divinely supported and held by Ryan even though I couldn't see, hear, touch, or smell him. Judy received my gratitude and started gathering the things she had placed on the table to find her tissues and placed them back in her pocketbook. It can be an extremely powerful and healing experience when we can connect and feel supported by our person that is no longer with us. "It was lovely meeting you, Whitney. I am so sorry for your loss, but you're going to be OK. More than OK. Trust that," she said as she reached out her hand to mine and gave it a quick and gentle squeeze. I smiled softly and nodded. "I'll walk you out," I said as I started to walk to the front door. Judy followed behind me. I opened the door and Judy walked through and onto the porch. The cool, refreshing breeze hit my face and the top of my chest that was exposed in the shirt I was wearing. I marveled at how beautiful an afternoon it was. "Drive safe!" I said as I waved goodbye. Judy smiled and waved back and then started walking away toward her car in the driveway. Before taking the step off of the porch, she turned around quickly and said, "Ryan wants you to know one more thing," she paused. I held my breath again as the lump in my throat returned. Judy continued, "You're going to meet someone and you're going to have one more baby and it will be a girl. He doesn't want you to feel guilty for opening up your heart to someone again. This baby's soul is waiting for the right time to join you and Ryan is telling her all about you," she smiled again and started walking off the porch. I stood almost in disbelief at what Judy had just said. It was one of the most sad and beautiful things I had ever heard. I pictured Ryan holding a sweet baby girl in his arms and telling her about me while smiling and laughing. "Thank you, Judy," I said as tears started rolling down my cheeks again and I shut the front door. I stared at the back of the door for a moment and stared at the glass panes twinkling as the sun hit them at different points as Judy's car backed up slowly from the driveway. Standing in the hallway after that reading with Judy, a sense of connectedness with Ryan, my future, and my destiny flooded over me. It was unmistakable. I knew what I was going to do next. Ryan had given me wings to fly and I was going to jump.

You Don't Have to Be "Woo-Woo," But It Helps

I almost didn't include this chapter in the book because I know there are some people who vehemently disagree with and don't believe in mediums or even in receiving signs from loved ones who have crossed over. However, I know there are many who can resonate and find comfort in me sharing this experience and I thought it was important to share this part of my grief journey because it has brought me a lot of peace, although I don't have an explanation for it. There have been events and phenomena since Ryan's accident that I cannot explain. There have been signs and feelings that cannot be analyzed through the lens of logic or reason. Like my encounter with Judy, there is so much that I don't understand, and events that I cannot deny happened. In all transparency, I am a Jewish woman, but I am not religious. I haven't been to synagogue in decades, probably since my youngest sister's bat mitzvah, but I believe strongly in God and Heaven. I would say I am very spiritual, and I am open to individuals possessing certain gifts like being able to talk to the dead and telling you things about your future. I am open to the possibilities because I have witnessed things that can only be reconciled with the belief that there is a force and power bigger than all of us somewhere. I also truly believe that our souls' journey doesn't end with our deaths on Earth. I believe that our loved ones who die still remain connected to us in some way and can show us signs in various forms. Being able to ask for signs from Ryan and receiving them back in a significant way throughout my grief journey since his death has been incredibly cathartic and validating for me. After Ryan sustained his brain injury I almost immediately began seeing the numbers "111," an angel number, everywhere. I caught the times 1:11 and 11:11 almost every day; I saw the numbers on billboards, stickers, and license plates. I originally believed it was a sign that Ryan would recover, but I know now it was him letting me know that no matter what, everything would be OK and that he would always be with us in some form. In my life now I tend to see "111" when I am struggling or questioning myself or right before something significant is going to happen in my life. Ryan always seems to know when to divinely support or celebrate me exactly when I need it the most. Believing and feeling that our relationship did not end with his death and that I will see him again in some form, someday brings me incredible solace. I am not asking you to believe what I believe. Maybe you think all of this is utter nonsense, and that's totally OK. You don't have to believe in mediums or tarot cards. My point is that finding an authentic way to feel connected to your person who died, perhaps through ritual, asking for signs, taking walks in nature, or meditating can help you through the depths of your suffering in grief. It can perhaps provide you with the faith that this isn't the end of your relationship with your person, the connection lives on after death, and one day you will be reunited. The belief that I will reunite with Ryan after I die is a conviction that I hold onto tightly and intimately. This hope and trust have rescued me from the darkest crevices of my sorrow and have allowed me to take steps forward in my new life more confidently and with more peace that Ryan is also on this journey with me, cheering me on, guiding me, and walking beside me before we meet again. The promise of Heaven is hopeful and beautiful, but I know in my heart that before that time I have so much left to live and people to love. I have come to realize that living with grief means intentionally firmly planting yourself in the process of living and finding meaning in this experience, although there will always be a pull from Heaven. How brave it is to fully embrace life and find joy when it means carrying the pain of our loss until our last breaths. This is both the burden and privilege of our life as grievers.

Connecting with Your Loved One

There are many ways to feel connected to someone you love who isn't physically here. I know it isn't the same at all. There is simply no substitute for our person being here physically doing life with us, and it can be frustrating when we can't seem to feel our person's presence when we so badly want to. Here are some ways to connect with your person that I hope brings some peace to your tender heart:

- Talk to your person or write to them.
- Think about what your person would say or do when you feel like you need their guidance, support, or advice.

- Get out in nature and appreciate the beauty in the world. For example, whenever I see a beautiful sunrise or sunset, I like to think Ryan is painting the sky for us.
- Carry on traditions that your person loved or create new traditions in their honor.
- Visit places they loved in life or visit places you always talked about going together.
- Do activities your person loved doing or do activities you talked about doing together.
- Carry on your person's legacy and memory by living life as your person did, with the same values and mantras.
- Tell stories about your person.
- Look at your person's pictures or watch videos of them.
- Practice being still with yourself and trying to connect with your person.
- Tell your person that you want to dream about them or that you want them to send you a specific sign.

11 | I Carry It All with Me

"Look at all the stars, mama!" Jackson says in a sweet and excited voice, leaning his head straight up toward the sky. I walk over to him, wrap my arms around his little chest from the back of his body, and kneel down to his level. I look up at the sky myself and see dozens of tiny sparkles of light. "Wow! Look at all of those! It is so beautiful, isn't it Jackson?" I ask with enthusiasm. "Mm-hmm," he answers. *The stars really are beautiful*, I think to myself, and my brain immediately flashes to Ryan. Thinking about where his spirit is. If he can see the stars too or if he is even part of the stars now. "You're so cute," I say looking down at Jackson, twirling him around, and grabbing his hand as we start walking down the final stretch of the street before reaching our new home of three months. We have adopted the new nightly ritual of taking family walks after dinner. It is a habit that we all look forward to and something that helps relax baby Leo before putting him down for the night to avoid any prolonged crying spells. I look up and around, admiring the lit-up houses in our neighborhood. It is fall again. The crispness in the air has returned, and although it is only 7:30 at night, the almost full moon is shining brightly against a black backdrop. I look over at Anthony, who is pushing Leo's stroller next to Jackson, and I smile at Leo's little baby legs and feet sticking out prominently at the bottom. Anthony looks over at Jackson and quickly scoops him up, wrapping his left arm around Jackson's torso. Jackson squeals and laughs in delight. Anthony continues to push the stroller and carry Jackson down the street. The sweet sight of Anthony loving my boys so well sends a surge of warmness to my heart. It makes me so happy to see my boys with a father that cares for them so well and fully as if they were his own children. I am in love with the man who is walking beside me with my most precious little beings in the world being held and pushed along by him. He brings me a sense of peace and comfort that I didn't think was possible after all the trauma I have been through. We are a family.

There is a predictable rhythm and pattern to our lives now that I yearned to regain after Ryan's accident and death. Doing the ordinary and mundane things in my everyday life with the people I love and cherish is what I missed the most when my world fell apart. Somehow I have gotten the simplistic beauty of a normal family life back. Yet it is not the same as it was. It is not the life that I thought I would be living. But I have found solace and happiness within this new existence. I feel content, secure, and grateful. This new life I have created in the wake of tragedy is magical all on its own. Yet within grief, so many things are true at once. This new life will always mean that I am not living my old life. It means that Ryan is dead. The heaviness in my heart no longer feels impossible to hold in my chest, but it has weight all the same. The weight serves as a reminder that there is love housed inside me for someone precious that was ripped away far too early, easily, and unfairly. You have also found yourself in a new life with a new identity that you never wanted or asked for and yet here you are. There are things in life that happen to us that cause us to break and question the point in all of this. You've probably asked yourself "why me?" or "why us?" on several occasions. There is no answer to this question other than death does not discriminate and doesn't care about how good your person was or the plans you had. It isn't fair and that is the harsh truth of life. You have to make the decision if you want to let this unfairness and darkness swallow you up or if you want to create something beautiful from it. It is your choice and your choice alone but your life will pass no matter what. Isn't it worth fighting for the good knowing that your time here is finite and precious?

You will carry your grief and the love for your person until your last breath. The intensity of the anguish you feel in the early aftermath of your loss can get incrementally better over time if you put in the work, but grief's resurgence is unpredictable. The pain will ebb and flow like the waves in the ocean. But it is possible to live through this forever process with more ease and grace. The waves will keep crashing, but they won't knock you down like they once did in the acute stages of grief. Your ability to withstand and integrate the weight of your loss requires intentionality. It requires surrendering to the pain that flows from your loss, leaning into the activities and people that bring you peace within your grief, discovering who you are in the world without your person, learning to love yourself as a person who has been transformed through tragedy, not allowing the opinions and actions/inactions of others to deter you from your path, finding a way to form a new type of connection with your person who is no longer here, and starting to build a life that feels authentic to you where joy and purpose can exist and grow. Grief can crush and swallow you up if you allow it to. I have prevented being consumed by Ryan's death and have found it tremendously helpful in my own grief to shift the goal for my grief from "getting rid of," "erasing," and "moving on from" to learning to live with and assimilating my pain. By simply shifting the goal in grief from feeling the need to extinguish it in order to continue living, to learning to live alongside the grief while moving forward, so much pressure has been lifted. This mindset is something I have learned on my own through my own grief experience and something I share with my grief coaching clients so they can stop judging themselves so harshly for thinking they aren't progressing well enough or fast enough in their own grief experience. I try to impress upon my clients that there isn't a destination in grief. There is no ending and thus no pressure to rush through it or do it better than someone else. I try to teach my clients to come to themselves and their grief like a practice each day. This gives them space and grace to come to living within the grief experience however they are on any given day, or any given moment, and then ask themselves, "How do I need to tend to myself and my grief today?" As grievers, we do not need to choose between carrying our grief and honoring our loss and experiencing joy and peace. All of these things are accessible to us and are part of us as grievers. I know I don't need to choose between honoring the sadness I feel from Ryan's death and mourning the life and future we were supposed to live together and also truly feeling like I am living in this new life with Anthony, my sons, and the people I love that are still here. The expectation that you should be magically better or healed from your grief and pain can hinder you from moving forward because it is unrealistic. You lost someone precious to you that cannot be replaced. The trauma and the tragedy you endured surrounding the death of your person is part of you now. This type of pain is not intended to be put down, forgotten, swept under the rug, or fixed. That is impossible. You aren't meant to fix something that is not broken. The grief and pain you feel from the death of your person is not wrong. After a life-altering loss multiple truths co-exist; you are meant to grieve the person you loved and lost for the rest of your life AND you can live a life you love even with this harsh reality. I've come to peace and accepted that the darkness I hold is a forever darkness. If you've lost someone precious, you also hold a darkness. But there is so much light in you too. The darkness is a weight we take up and endure for our lifetime and is intricately intertwined with the love for our person. These things can never be separated. The pain will be forever present, but it doesn't have to be all there is. It doesn't have to completely consume your world. You have to be brave enough to start imagining life anew and taking intentional steps forward to create a reality that is beautiful and good without your person. Life will never feel or look the same as it once did when your person was alive, but relief, magic, and love can still be found here, in life with grief. Ask yourself, in this new reality and world, what does a beautiful life look like for me?

***

I crawl into bed next to Anthony, who is quietly scrolling on his phone in the dark, and I pull the heavy white comforter over my legs and up to my shoulders. I still feel cold from the chilly air from our walk earlier. My legs ache from my morning workout and I lean my head back, sink the back of my body into my pillow, and let out a big sigh. My body feels exhausted. My mind and spirit feel worn out. It is the fall season of 2023 and with it brings the second anniversary of Ryan's accident and a resurgence of my grief. My loss is far more palpable this time of year. My entire being feels like it is preparing to fight for Ryan's life like I did on the day of his accident, except I don't have to fight anymore. I am safe and in bed with the man I love on Earth, and my whole being feels the gravity from Heaven is pulling me toward it, where a part of me will reside for eternity. Needless to say, I have been difficult to be around. I've been anxious, and restless, my mind foggy and forgetful, and I've been short-tempered. Anthony has been taking the brunt of the manifestation of my grief, which always seems to come out in the form of edginess versus despair. I know what is on the other side of the "wanting to crawl of out my skin feeling" and wanting to scream at every well-meaning person that does even the slightest thing to piss me off, like drive slowly. On the other side of my anger and frustration is that gut-wrenching feeling of my person being dead. The memories of my life with Ryan are so much on the surface that it feels like I'm touching them most times of the day now. The memories of his accident, his time in the hospital, and his death are also right on the surface. And I don't know what thoughts are more painful to think about: thinking about the beautiful life that I had with Ryan that I can never have again or of the traumas I endured along with Ryan's suffering, deterioration, and death. So many layers of grief, each placed one on top of the other.

Anthony and I had an honest and heartfelt conversation about how I was acting and I was reminded how calm and rational he is even when it feels like I have very little control over my own erratic emotions that come with waves of grief. Our relationship isn't all rainbows and butterflies. It is far from a fairy tale. It takes work to find common ground and understanding when there are young children to parent, a dead husband, three families involved instead of just two, and the mess of complexities that comes with that. But there is so much love and devotion between us even when things get hard and messy. Our partnership is solid and real like my marriage was with Ryan. Anthony is my person now, my anchor through any storm. He willingly and thoughtlessly holds so much of my darkness to make space for the light within me to shine. He is our angel on Earth.

With no words left between us for the evening, I inch closer to Anthony in bed and nestle into the warmth of his body, landing my head on top of his chest. I wrap my one leg around the bottom of his legs and close my eyes trying to steady my uneasy mind. I focus on Anthony's heartbeat thumping in his chest and think about listening to Ryan's heartbeat as I laid in bed with him during hospice in the days before he died. I tried to memorialize the sound and feel of Ryan's beating heart against my cheek and ears. I remember feeling sad that I may forget this part of him. But I hadn't forgotten and now I don't believe I ever will. Ryan's heartbeat was slow and forceful while Anthony's heartbeat is quicker and gentle. Two different men, two distinct hearts and beats, two different distinct lives, but a love for me, Jackson, and Leo is the connection between us through Heaven and Earth.

I drift off to sleep easily that night to the sound of Anthony's heartbeat and the comfort of his body, feeling like something had been lifted from me. And that same fall night that we took our family walk and my heart exploded seeing Anthony interact with my boys, and Jackson told me to look up at the stars, is the same night I had my second dream of Ryan since his death. The first dream had happened well over a year after Ryan died and I was in the bedroom of our old home. Ryan was right below my bedroom window looking up at me and smiling. He was dressed in his police uniform, hat, and all. In the dream, my bedroom door was open and I felt the urge to run to him, but I couldn't leave my bedroom. I was cemented to that place, looking at Ryan smiling at me from afar. He didn't say any words, but he was completely healed and looked at peace. I felt his love even though he couldn't say the words, "I love you." I remember waking up from that dream and feeling a sense that Ryan was OK wherever he was. I took the dream to mean that although I couldn't talk to Ryan, touch him, or even feel him with me all the time, he was still always with me and the boys. It was incredibly comforting.

The second dream was different. More intense and vivid. Ryan and I embraced in this second dream, our reunion after our time separated by death. Again, his smile was so big and the look of utter bliss and contentment never changed from his face in the course of the dream. He was in a white t-shirt and his skin glowed, a soft light emanating from every inch of him. Ryan was such a beautiful man in life, but in this dream, he was the most beautiful I had ever seen him. This time in the dream, he spoke to me, telling me to come with him. He laughed and pulled my hand to follow him. I felt my desire to just surrender and run away with him wherever he would take me. But like in my first dream, I felt cemented to where I was planted. "I can't go with you. I have so much left to do. There are so many people I love here. Our boys need me," I said as if even trying to convince myself. I felt like there was a tug-of-war between my life on Earth and what could be my life in Heaven with Ryan. Ryan stopped pulling me in the dream and he took me in to hold me. I didn't want him to leave but it was a quick embrace and he started to walk away. "You're right Boo. It's not your time. You have so much left to do. I'll be here waiting for you. I love you," he said confidently, still smiling as he walked away into a huge bright light that swallowed him up as he instantly disappeared.

I woke up with a start. The sun was just starting to appear through the large windows in the bedroom causing a soft, warm light to envelop the room. There was a hollow space next to me where Anthony had slept, but he had already gotten up early for the day to go to the gym and get ready for work. The dream with Ryan had left me feeling more connected to him and even more certain that one day I would see him again. But it also solidified what I have known so confidently since the day that he died. I am meant to have a meaningful, purposeful, and beautiful life without him before we meet again. Ryan's death was the end of our journey together on Earth, but it was just the beginning of the next part of my life that I was destined to live without him. My life and the achievements I am supposed to accomplish, the impact I am supposed to have in people's lives, the experiences I am supposed to have, and the people that I am supposed to love in my lifetime did not end with Ryan's last breath. I am still here. In this next chapter of life, I house pain and longing that I didn't have in my old life, but I'm using these emotions to fuel me to live each and every day to the best of my abilities knowing that my time here is fragile and temporary. I'm using them as a reminder that we are never guaranteed any next moment and to embrace all the good this world has to offer while I have the opportunity. It is what Ryan would want for me and our boys. To live fully and love fiercely while we are here. It doesn't mean that my loss is easy to carry, but my desire not to waste this one precious life we are given being suffocated and crushed by what has been taken from me far outweighs the darkness. The light I still possess shines though. *And the light YOU possess shines through too.* It is what lifts me up when I am being pulled down by the grief. I will always feel a tug from Heaven because Ryan is there waiting for me, but I am exactly where I am supposed to be. I will hold the pain of losing Ryan while I also hold the love we shared into this next season and new chapter of my life until the day I die. My love for Ryan is intertwined in each step forward I take. It is part of life now as there is no life without grief but there is much more to my world now. I am meant to build something special in the place I am firmly planted with the people I am planted with, living within a world that contains grief. I will never live in a world that isn't complex and complicated, one that isn't twisted and mangled with my loss. If you've lost someone precious like I have, you also will never live in a world without the feelings and energy of your loss. But remember there is still beauty here and a meaningful life left to live. The love, sorrow, beauty, mess, triumph, defeat, light, darkness, endings, and beginnings are all part of me after the death of my person as they are all part of you as well. I carry all of these with me now and yet, it all feels lighter because my life is so much more than just what I have lost, it is about what and who I've gained in the process of rising from the wreckage. My hope for you is that the pain that flows from your loss will get lighter as well, as you build an authentically beautiful life and hold what now must be carried.

An Activity to Leave You With

I want you to imagine yourself with whatever weight you have been carrying since your person died or WHEN the world as you KNEW it shattered into a million little unrecognizable pieces. That weight may be pain. It may be fear, guilt, shame, loneliness, doubt, the expectations of others, the new mental load of life without your person, or all of the above. I want you to imagine yourself with all that heaviness and the resistance that weight is causing you—making it difficult for you to move forward in life and find joy, peace, and purpose again. The resistance you imagine can look like a boulder you are carrying or a big, heavy backpack. Whatever works for you so you can imagine being weighed down. Then I want you to imagine another version of yourself. The other version of yourself doesn't need the resistance anymore to protect you and can release the burden of it all. What does this version of you look like? What does this version of you feel like? Do you feel physically lighter? Are you happier? Are you smiling and laughing? Are you more grateful or passionate about life? Then envision the old version of yourself hugging the new you and saying the following:

> "Thank you for getting me to this place. For surviving. For getting up each day even though it has been painful and heavy. But this weight is holding you back from thriving and living a life you love. You deserve happiness. You deserve peace. You deserve laughter and pure joy. You deserve love. You don't need this part of us anymore. This is where we say goodbye."

Now go out and live a big, beautiful life.

Afterword

My promise to you, my reader, at the beginning of this book, was that if you were intentional about incorporating the tools, strategies, and perspectives that I learned after my husband's death—that have allowed me to hold and carry my pain in the world while still feeling like I am living—that the pain you are feeling right now wouldn't always feel so heavy. I stand by that promise, but I also want you to understand that healing does not happen in a vacuum and that navigating the harsh and messy terrain of deep grief after the death of someone you love, like a spouse, cannot be done in isolation.

The day after Ryan's accident, I knew that the intensity of the despair that ravaged my body, mind, and spirit was much bigger than me. Even in complete shock after the worst day of my life, I intuitively knew that I could not manage and make sense of all the pain I was feeling by myself. I reached out immediately to find someone who specialized in grief and trauma to help guide me through this process. For almost two years, every week, I sat for an hour at a time with a trusted professional and talked about what I was going through. Grief and trauma are so overwhelming and you need someone to extract the thoughts and feelings that you cannot make sense of, so you can start processing the enormity of the experience that you have survived. An outsider who knows how to sit and witness your great pain and give perspective on an experience that has shattered your world in every aspect is invaluable and powerful. I would not have found the peace and joy I have been able to discover without having that soft place to land my darkest thoughts, feelings, and memories. You need a soft place to land too.

Through my work as a certified grief coach and educator, I became the person that I needed when I was going through the worst days of my life. The sad reality is that there are not many individuals who specialize in helping those in grief. This work is extremely rewarding, but at the same time can be mentally and emotionally taxing, which is why not many individuals decide to devote their lives to this work. For me, it is a calling and something I feel I must do in order to fulfill the purpose that I was put on this Earth to do. Today I offer one-on-one grief support for those who have suffered any life-altering loss, meaning any loss that feels profound and life-changing to the griever. My coaching is for those who need to be fully witnessed in their pain, who need additional support and guidance to make sense of a world that no longer makes sense without their person, and who want to start feeling like they are living and embracing life again instead of just going through life on autopilot. I guide my clients through all of the struggles that are talked about in this book (and more) including managing the physical items of loved ones, how to become your own form of comfort and safety when all the support fades, finding your identity after loss, navigating dating and finding love after the death of a spouse, the complexities of relationships after a death, how to tap into your spirituality, how to process pain and anger, and how to move through the typical roadblocks in grief, including guilt, that are preventing a griever from moving forward. I want to remind you again that you aren't meant to move through the experience of your profound loss and pain by yourself and if you need more support after you close the pages of this book, I'd be honored to be your guide on this journey with you. Learning to carry everything you are holding right now with more grace and ease is not easy. In fact, I am sure it feels impossible right now, and I want you to know how brave you are for even reading this book and looking forward to a scary and unknown future. Below are ways to contact me directly to get further grief support from someone who has walked the same path you are on right now and who intimately knows the pain you carry. You are not alone.

Take the next step by reaching out:
My website: www.whitneylynallen.com
My email: whitneylallen12@gmail.com
Connect with me on social media @whitneylyn allen

Acknowledgments

This book would simply not have been possible without the guidance and belief of several individuals and entities. I would first like to thank Ashley Mansour and her team at Brands Through Books for helping me write a solid manuscript for this book to make it possible to cross over into the traditional publishing space. I would also like to thank Ashley and her team for their expertise in querying publishers to make my dream of being a traditionally published author a reality.

I would also like to thank everyone at Wiley for believing in me, the grief work I do in the world, and of course for believing this book would help so many people. It is not lost on me that many people do not get the opportunity to have a team of experts behind them when trying to get their ideas out into the world in book form, and I am forever grateful for the expertise and guidance of the Wiley team for making my dream a reality.

To my grief coaching clients for always inspiring me to become a better coach and mentor and to provide more practical, tangible, and implementable grief resources for grievers. Thank you for motivating me and being my "why" when I felt overwhelmed or defeated during the process of writing this book and getting it out into the world to serve you and others.

And of course on the home front, this book would not have been possible without my husband, Anthony, and my two sons, Jackson and Leo. Thank you for believing in me and my big dreams. This book would not be here without your unwavering love and support.

About
the Author

Whitney Lyn Allen Gadecki currently lives in Bucks County, Pennsylvania, with her husband, Anthony, and two sons, Jackson and Leo. Whitney's world was flipped upside down when her late husband, Ryan, had a severe reaction to a bee sting and sustained a severe brain injury, resulting in his death in April 2022. Since that time, the once practicing medical malpractice defense attorney followed her new calling to serve others who are also experiencing grief and trauma and share her vulnerable and personal grief journey with others. Whitney is a certified grief educator and provides grief coaching to those who are ready for their transformation and growth after loss. She is also the author of the memoir *Running in Trauma Stilettos*, which is an Amazon Best Seller. Whitney is so proud that her second book, *What Must Be Carried*, is out in the world to expand on her own grief process and provide a guide to start living again for those who have lost someone they love. Her goal is to continue to share the empowering message that there is so much beauty in life, even after the death of a loved one.